ONE
DIRECTION

ONE DIRECTION

SARAH OLIVER

JOHN BLAKE

Published by John Blake Publishing Ltd,
3 Bramber Court, 2 Bramber Road,
London W14 9PB, England

www.johnblakepublishing.co.uk

First published in paperback in 2011

ISBN: 978 1 84358 378 3

British Library Cataloguing-in-Publication Data:

A catalogue record for this book is available from the British Library.

Design by www.envydesign.co.uk

Printed and bound by CPI Group (UK) Ltd, Croydon, CR0 4YY

7 9 10 8

Papers used by John Blake Publishing are natural, recyclable products made
from wood grown in sustainable forests. The manufacturing processes
conform to the environmental regulations of the country of origin.

All photographs reproduced courtesy of WENN

Dedicated with love to David, James, Tom,
Megan, Adam and Joshua.

INTRODUCTION

The *One Direction A–Z* is jam-packed with everything you need to know about the UK's newest boy band. No other book goes into so much detail or tells all the secrets from *The X Factor* live shows and what really went on when the cameras weren't rolling. Read all about the chilli challenge, how they came up with their name and what the boys look for in a girl.

Find out what pranks the boys have pulled on each other and why Harry owes everything to his best friend, Will.

Sarah Oliver is a celebrity journalist who knows more about One Direction than any other journalist on the planet. She has worked with One Direction's closest friends, who have been supporting Harry, Liam, Louis, Niall and Zayn since the very beginning.

You can follow Sarah on Twitter (http://Twitter.com/SarahOliverAtoZ). This is the fifth book in the *A–Z* series so why not check out the *Robert Pattinson A–Z*, *Taylor Lautner A–Z*, *The Completely Unofficial Glee A–Z* or *The Wanted A–Z*?

You can read this book from start to finish, or dip in and out of it, as you prefer.

A is for...

Accidents

Liam, Zayn, Harry, Niall and Louis might not have been together for long but they have already experienced an accident or two. Their first accident was during the Judges' Houses round when they were preparing to sing for Simon Cowell and Sinitta. Poor Louis managed to get stung by a sea urchin and was rushed to hospital in Spain as his foot began to swell.

In the last week of October the boys were enjoying a night off with Mary Byrne and Cher Lloyd when Liam hurt himself. They had all gone to see the rapper Tinie Tempah perform at Koko in Camden, North London. The boys were enjoying being in the VIP booth with

HARRY AND THE BOYS ALWAYS LIKE TO HAVE FUN AND MESS AROUND WHEN THEY'RE NOT PERFORMING OR MEETING THEIR FANS.

Kimberley Walsh, Nicola Roberts and Chipmunk, not knowing what was about to happen to Liam. Tinie Tempah was glad to see the band and called them onstage. Somehow Liam managed to trip over when he tried to step around a guitar pedal. He twisted his ankle but had to pretend that everything was okay. Thankfully, the adrenaline kicked in and Liam jumped around the stage with the other lads because he was keen to make a good impression on the hundreds of people watching and didn't want to create a fuss.

Liam ended up having to be helped to the car by *X Factor* minders because he couldn't walk by himself, but he couldn't afford to take things easy and so the next day he was up and about again. He rehearsed with the others but had to sit down while the others stood. Having an injury was frustrating for him because it restricted what he was able to do.

Thankfully, no serious damage was done and so by the time Saturday night came, he was able to perform although painkillers and heavy strapping definitely helped. Even if he had broken his leg, he would have insisted on performing; he didn't want to let Zayn, Harry, Niall and Louis down. Their Halloween themed performance started with the lads sitting on steps and then they stood up and moved towards the judges. It's clear that Liam was in pain during 'Total Eclipse of the Heart' but because it was Halloween Week it simply looked as if he was playing the part of a zombie.

The third accident happened when Harry and the rest of the boys were trying to get through a big crowd of fans. They had just got out of a car and were heading for the studio door when Harry was knocked over by some fans. They didn't mean to do it, but as soon as

Harry went down, Liam shouted over to check that his band mate was okay. He wanted to help him up, but he couldn't do so because of the sheer number of fans in the way. In the end, Harry managed to stand up with help and carried on smiling – he must have been so relieved by the time he got inside.

NIALL AND LOUIS 'SMILE' FOR THE CAMERAS!

Aiden Grimshaw

Eighteen-year-old Aiden Grimshaw from Blackpool was one of the boys' closest friends in the *X Factor* house until he was voted off in Week Six. They had been close since Boot Camp. Like One Direction, Aiden had been one of the favourites to win and so everyone was shocked when Dermot O'Leary announced that he was in the bottom two with Katie Waissel.

While Katie and Aiden prepared to sing for survival during the advertising break, Louis from the band went on Twitter. He tweeted: 'What a joke, Wagner through and not Aiden!!! Aiden has to get through!!!!'

In a matter of minutes it became the top tweet when anyone searched for Wagner as it was re-tweeted by lots of people. Sadly for Louis, the judges failed to save Aiden and after Walsh took it to deadlock, it was revealed that Katie had secured the most votes.

Meanwhile Louis kept on tweeting, not seeming to care if he got in trouble. He tweeted: 'Not only was he one of my best friends, he was one of the best singers in the competition, yet people who can't sing a note in tune are still here. Wow.'

Liam joined in to say: 'Aiden didn't deserve that.'

The boys were so upset for their friend but they weren't the only ones. Dannii Minogue, Aiden's mentor, tweeted: 'My utmost respect to Aiden. I have loved working with him on X Factor. TeamMinogue will miss him and I wish him the VERY BEST! Dx'

Rather than wanting to attack Wagner, Louis and Liam were angrier about the situation. Only a few weeks earlier, Liam had told his local paper, *The Express and Star*: 'I think everyone deserves their place in their own little way in *X Factor* because it is not just a

X FACTOR CONTESTANT AND ONE DIRECTION FRIEND, AIDEN GRIMSHAW.

singing competition, otherwise it would be called something else. He [Wagner] brings different things to the show. Everyone has got a guilty pleasure for Wagner as well.'

Since Aiden moved out of the *X Factor* house, the boys have stayed in touch with him and promoted a petition to make sure their friend would be included on The *X Factor* Live Tour. There was talk that he wasn't going to be asked and Louis invited all One Direction fans to join the petition to make sure that Aiden was part of it because he deserved to be there. And on 18

November, it was revealed that Aiden and the eight remaining acts would be performing on the tour. #aidenisonthetour quickly became a trending topic on Twitter, worldwide.

American Anthems – Week Five

The fifth week of the *X Factor* live shows saw the ten remaining acts sing American anthems. That week, the boys talked to Simon a lot about their ambition to win the competition. He thought 'Kids In America' was the perfect song for them and that their version could be a hit single as it was that good in rehearsals.

WHO SANG WHAT

Aiden Grimshaw – 'Nothing Compares 2 U' by Prince

Matt Cardle – 'The First Time Ever I Saw Your Face' by Roberta Flack

Paije Richardson – Mash up of 'I'm a Believer' by The Monkees and 'Hey Ya!' by Outkast

Treyc Cohen – 'I Don't Want to Miss a Thing' by Aerosmith

Rebecca Ferguson – 'Make You Feel My Love' by Bob Dylan

Katie Waissel – 'Don't Speak' by No Doubt

Cher Lloyd – 'Empire State of Mind' by Jay-Z
and Alicia Keys
Mary Byrne – 'There You'll Be' by Faith Hill
Wagner – Mash up of 'Viva Las Vegas' and 'The
Wonder Of You' by Elvis Presley
One Direction – 'Kids In America' by Kim Wilde

WHAT THE JUDGES THOUGHT OF ONE DIRECTION'S PERFORMANCE

Louis Walsh: 'What a brilliant way to end the show! Listen, everywhere I go there's hysteria, it's building on this band. You remind me a bit of Westlife, Take That, Boyzone... you could be the next big band. I loved everything about the performance, but Simon, Simon, one point... I have to get my rulebook out: the theme is 'American Anthems' – this wasn't even a hit in America! It's by Kim Wilde from London – it's not an American anthem, so you cheated. Your mentor has cheated!'

ONE DIRECTION WERE FANS OF WAGNER, SAYING THAT EACH ACT BROUGHT SOMETHING DIFFERENT TO THE SHOW.

Dannii Minogue: 'It had the word "America" in it, and it had American cheerleaders and it was a great performance, guys. I don't think, vocally, it was the best of the night but a great performance!'

Cheryl Cole: 'That absolutely cheered me up and brightened up my night, I thoroughly enjoyed that performance. You are great kids: I love chatting to you backstage, you are just good lads, nice lads. Great performance, good song choice, Cowell, I've got to give it to you but it isn't American all the same.'

Simon Cowell: 'When you came out, it was like sunshine on a beautiful day – and I've said this before, and then "Louis the Thundercloud" comes along and dribbles on everything that is happy. Taking all that rubbish to one side because it was about the artist, it was about song title, that was without question your best performance by a mile.'

WHAT THE BOYS THOUGHT

The boys loved performing 'Kids In America' and found it really fun. They enjoyed having the cheerleaders with them – even though it was a bit of a headache for the *X Factor*'s stylists, who had to make 35 cheerleader outfits. And they were so thankful to Brian Friedman, who created the fantastic choreography.

Liam, Louis, Zayn, Niall and Harry hadn't been sure on the song at the start of the week and it took a few

Not for the first time, X Factor judge Louis Walsh paid the ultimate compliment to One Direction by comparing them to Boy Band gods, Take That!

rehearsals for them to feel confident. There had also been a lot of pressure placed on them because they would be singing last and people wanted a big performance to close the show.

THE SING-OFF

Katie and Treyc received the lowest number of votes and so they had to sing for survival. First, Katie sang 'Please Don't Give Up On Me' by Solomon Burke and then Treyc sang Toni Braxton's 'Un-break My Heart'. Simon voted to send Treyc home, Cheryl controversially refused to vote, Dannii voted to send Katie home and Louis also voted to send Treyc home.

And so Treyc became the seventh act to leave the show.

BRIAN FRIEDMAN IS THE RESIDENT CHOREOGRAPHER FOR *THE X FACTOR*.

Auditions

Our five favourite lads all auditioned to be solo artists. They came from different parts of England (and Ireland) and didn't even get to meet each other until Boot Camp.

Louis auditioned in Manchester and was one of the last people to be put through to Boot Camp. Sadly his audition wasn't shown on *The X Factor* or *Xtra Factor* shows. It's a real shame that the first time we got to hear him sing was at the Judges' Houses. He's a talented vocalist and if you want to hear his versions of Chris Brown's 'Crawl', Ne-Yo's 'Because Of You' and the Black Eyed Peas' 'I Gotta Feeling', you need to visit his YouTube channel: http://www.youtube.com/user/louistomlinson07. You can also see two videos of Louis playing Danny Zuko in his high-school production of *Grease*.

Zayn's auditions were also missed from the *X Factor* and *Xtra Factor* audition shows, which must have been disappointing for him and his family. Some One Direction fans have started an online petition to get Zayn's and Louis' auditions aired on TV or at least placed on YouTube. Right now, Zayn doesn't have an official YouTube channel and if you search for his audition, then you are directed to a racist video of people pretending to be Zayn, so be careful that you don't get tricked into clicking on it.

SADLY FOR THE ONE DIRECTION BOYS, TREYC COHEN WAS VOTED OFF *THE X FACTOR* IN WEEK 5.

Zayn admitted to the *Telegraph & Argus* newspaper that he actually auditioned for the show in 2009, but he was just too nervous and walked away. The same thing almost happened again, but this time his mum Tricia wouldn't let him give up. Zayn explained: 'I was really nervous, but she told me just to get on with it and not miss my chance.' It's a good job Zayn's mum pushed him, otherwise he might have missed out on the opportunity to be in One Direction.

Like Louis, Harry auditioned in Manchester but his audition was shown on the main *X Factor* show. Like many others, he was earmarked early on for the live shows. Harry's friends and family attended the audition with him. They wore T-shirts with 'We Think Harry Has The X Factor' on the front of them. The men had black T-shirts and the women wore white ones to make themselves stand out from the crowd and let Harry know how much they were willing him on. They wanted to be there to help him through the long day ahead. When you audition for *The X Factor* you have to queue for hours and before you get to audition for the judges, there are a few rounds in front of other *X Factor* staff. They pick only the very best (and sometimes the very worst) to go in front of Simon Cowell, Louis and co.

Harry had wanted to audition for the show before but he had been too young. He must have been so happy on his sixteenth birthday because he knew that he would now be able to audition. Harry admitted to Dermot O'Leary in his first *X Factor* interview: 'People tell me I'm a good singer – it's usually my mum [pointing to his proud mum who was standing right next to him]. Singing is what I want to do!'

When he was called to go on stage, Harry got a kiss on the cheek from his mum and a kiss on the head from his mate. Dermot even asked if anyone else wanted to kiss him!

Harry might have been nervous but the audience loved him straightaway. He didn't even have to start singing – they just started to cheer. He had picked Stevie Wonder's 'Isn't She Lovely' for his audition song. It was an unusual song choice for someone of his age. By the time he finished, Harry had the audience spellbound – and guest judge Nicole Scherzinger was totally smitten!

WHAT THE JUDGES SAID
Nicole Scherzinger: 'I'm really glad that we had the opportunity to hear you a cappella 'cos we could really hear how great your voice is. For sixteen years old, you have a beautiful voice.'

Louis Walsh: 'I agree with Nicole… however, I think you're so young. I don't think you have enough experience or confidence yet.'

Harry had guest judge Nicole Scherzinger totally smitten when he auditioned in Manchester.

Simon Cowell: '[Talking to Louis] Someone in the audience just said "rubbish" and I totally agree with them because the show is designed to find someone, whether you're fifteen, sixteen, seventeen, it doesn't matter. I think with a bit of vocal coaching, you could actually be very good.'

When it came to casting votes, Louis said: 'Harry, for all the right reasons I am going to say no.' Meanwhile, Simon Cowell was so disgusted with Louis's rejection that he encouraged the audience to boo him louder – even Harry joined in with a 'boo'. Nicole and Simon Cowell both said yes, so he made it through to Boot Camp.

Backstage, Harry's ecstatic mum gave Dermot a kiss!

Niall had a long wait before he got to meet the judges. With thousands of other hopefuls, he queued up at Croke Park Stadium in Dublin, survived the first round and was told to come back the next day. He then had two more auditions in front of X Factor staff, was interviewed by Dermot and told they would be in touch. A month later, when he was on holiday in Spain he got a phone call to tell him that he would be auditioning in front of Simon, Cheryl, Louis and Katy Perry. Many fans of The X Factor don't realise the long process that is involved when someone wants to audition. At any step along the way, Niall could have been rejected and he would have missed out.

X Factor PRESENTER DERMOT O'LEARY.

In fact, his actual audition in front of the main judges didn't go fantastically well but he still managed to scrape through. That audition didn't make the *X Factor* main show but was instead shown on the *Xtra Factor*. Niall was pretty confident when he was interviewed beforehand and revealed that people had compared him to Justin Bieber in the past. He admitted: 'I want to sell out arenas, and make an album and work with some of the best artists in the world. Today is the start of it all – if I get through today, it's game on!' When Louis asked why he was auditioning, Niall said that he wanted to be the best artist he could be in the world. Unlike Harry, who had to audition in front of Louis, Nicole and Simon Cowell, Niall had four judges to impress: Louis, Simon, Cheryl Cole and Katy Perry. The audience wolf-whistled, took to their feet and cheered for him, but the judges were not convinced that his performance of Ne-Yo's 'So Sick' was good enough.

WHAT THE JUDGES SAID

Katy Perry: 'I think you're adorable! You've got charisma – I just think that maybe you should work on that. You're only sixteen: I started out when I was fifteen and I didn't make it until I was twenty-three.'

Simon Cowell: 'I think you're unprepared: I think you came with the wrong song, you're not as good as you thought you were, but I still like you.'

Cheryl Cole: 'Yeah, you're obviously adorable: you've got a lot of charm for a sixteen-year-old, but the song was too big for you, babe.'

Louis Walsh: 'No, I think you've got something. I think that people would absolutely like you because you're likeable.'

When it came to voting, Simon said yes, Cheryl was a 'no' and then Louis butted in with a 'yes' before Katy could cast her vote. He probably guessed that she was going to say no, but causing her to vote last would make her decide Niall's fate. It proved a very clever move as Katy felt torn, but eventually she said: 'You're in!' At this, Niall jumped in the air before rushing off to see his family. Katy's final words to him were, 'Don't let us down!'

Out of all the One Direction boys, Liam had the best

audition. He had auditioned before, back in 2008, and so he had some idea of what to expect from the judges but he hadn't had to audition in front of hundreds of people before and so that was a new experience. When he was interviewed queuing before his audition, it was clear that Liam didn't hold anything against Simon for not picking him at the Judges' Houses round in 2008. He understands now that he just wasn't ready and that Simon was right to tell him to get his GCSEs and come back in two years' time. Clearly, Simon had his best interests at heart.

Liam was very brave to audition again because he had experienced the pain of being twice rejected and he might have been rejected again. Last time he had been told at Boot Camp that he hadn't made it only for Simon to change his mind and put him through. Then, at Judges' Houses, he was told 'no' again. At his 2010 first audition, Liam admitted: 'I feel like today is my chance to prove to Simon Cowell that I have got what it takes. It would mean more than anything to get a "yes" off Simon Cowell today.'

As soon as he took to the stage, Simon immediately recognised him and Liam even commented that he hadn't seen him in a while.

OPPOSITE: ALTHOUGH NIALL'S ORIGINAL *X FACTOR* AUDITION DIDN'T GO COMPLETELY TO PLAN, HIS CHARISMA AND SELF-BELIEF SAW HIM THROUGH IN THE END.

Liam picked 'Cry Me A River' to sing and Cheryl wrongly thought that he would be singing the Justin Timberlake song. Instead, Liam sang the classic blues ballad of the same name written by Arthur Hamilton, made famous by Julie London in 1955 and more recently, performed by Michael Bublé and Susan Boyle. When Liam first auditioned, he sang Frank Sinatra's 'Fly Me to the Moon' – he found out then that Simon Cowell loves Swing and so the judges might have expected him to pick another unusual song for a boy of his age to tackle.

Liam hadn't even finished his song before the audience, Simon Cowell and guest judge Natalie Imbruglia took to their feet. He was amazing and everyone felt moved by his performance. Unlike so many other auditionees, Liam didn't just stand in one place, he moved around and made the stage his own.

WHAT THE JUDGES SAID

Cheryl: 'You've definitely got it; whatever it is, you've got it. And I thought your voice was really powerful.'

Natalie Imbruglia: 'That was really impressive, really, really impressive. I think other people in this competition should be a little bit worried about you. You're really good.'

Louis Walsh: 'I'm really glad that you came back. It was a brilliant, brilliant vocal and for sixteen years, it

LIAM HAD THE
SMOOTHEST *X FACTOR*
AUDITION OF ALL THE
ONE DIRECTION BOYS.

was so confident – you totally delivered. [Looking at Simon] Simon, this is the guy you didn't put through!'

Simon Cowell: 'He wasn't quite ready when he came to my house, two years ago. But I said to him then: "Come back, two years' time and you're going to be a different person." I got it right!'

Louis is funny when he tries to stir up trouble. Somehow Simon always seems to end up on top.

When it came to voting, the judges all agreed that Liam had something special and each of them gave him a 'yes'. Simon even went so far as to say: 'Based on talent, absolutely incredible, one massive, fat, almighty "yes,"' and gave him both thumbs up. Two years earlier, Simon had given Liam a more reluctant 'yes' at his very first audition: he had said that Liam's performance needed to be more fun and lacked, '20 per cent.' What a difference a couple of years make.

Liam couldn't contain his excitement and once he'd received a hug and a kiss from his mum, he went into the *X Factor* booth to express how he was feeling. He told the camera: 'I never expected in my wildest dreams for that to happen and to get that reaction. You know, it was so amazing. Simon stood up for me and that's just the most amazing thing in the world ever!'

B is for...

Beatles – Week Seven

The seventh week of *The X Factor* live shows saw the eight remaining acts sing Beatles songs.

Shortly before One Direction's performance, Liam told the official site: 'I'm a massive fan of The Beatles and I'm really looking forward to tonight. Although it's an oldie, we're going to make the song we sing tonight feel current. It's a complicated performance for us, full of harmonies and ad-libs, but it's the sort of performance that I think you'd expect from a top boy band. We're feeling the pressure a bit but if it all goes to plan, it'll be awesome!'

WHO SANG WHAT

Matt Cardle – 'Come Together'

Paije Richardson – 'Let It Be'

Rebecca Ferguson – 'Yesterday'

Katie Waissel – 'Help!'

Cher Lloyd – 'Imagine' (by John Lennon)

Wagner – A mash up of 'Get Back', 'Hippy Hippy Shake' and 'Hey Jude'

Mary Byrne – 'Something'

One Direction – 'All You Need Is Love'

WHAT THE JUDGES SAID

Louis Walsh: 'Hey, One Direction, thank God for you guys! You lifted the whole energy in the studio… good to see the Fab Five singing the Fab Four. The hysteria here has lifted your game: you are in it for the long haul, yes!'

Dannii Minogue: 'Guys, another fantastic performance. I've always given you good comments: I just have to say tonight, you guys [Niall and Zayn], were struggling. I don't know if it was caught on-camera, but you were struggling with the backing vocals. You didn't know if you were coming in or out. Don't let the other guys down, you have to work as a group.'

Cheryl Cole: 'I could get into the whole, "I don't know why your mentor put you on a plain platform like that", but I won't because above everything else, that was another great performance from you guys.'

Simon Cowell: 'Who cares about the platform? Can I just say, guys: as always, you worked hard, delivered a fantastic, unique version of the song and please for anyone at home who saw what happened last week, please don't think these guys are safe. This lot [Louis, Dannii and Cheryl] do not want you to do well in the competition. *I* do… please vote!'

Cheryl's comment about the platform was all because Simon had criticised her decision to place Cher Lloyd on a staircase for her earlier performance of 'Imagine'. One Direction didn't deserve to be brought into their petty squabble, though.

WHAT THE BOYS THOUGHT

Niall really enjoyed the performance and thought it their best yet. Liam told the backstage camera: 'Dannii gave us a bad comment, but we're going to get bad comments so we've just got to take it on board and improve it next week.'

The boys didn't really mind that Dannii had criticised them. As they survived each week in the competition, they knew that the other judges would start making bad comments because the boys threatened to knock out their acts.

THE SING-OFF

Katie Waissel and Paije Richardson received the lowest number of votes and so they had to sing for survival. Katie sang 'Stay' by Shakespears Sister and Paije performed Sam Brown's 'Stop!' Simon, Cheryl and Louis all voted to send Paije home and only Dannii voted for Katie.

And so Paije became the ninth act to leave the show.

Belle Amie

Belle Amie were the girl band put together by the judges at Boot Camp and they also made it to the live shows in Simon Cowell's group category. Sophia Wardman, Esther Campbell, Geneva Lane and Rebecca Creighton would have loved to become as popular as One Direction, but their *X Factor* journey had ended by Week Four.

The girls are friends of Harry, Liam, Zayn, Niall and Louis, but they aren't afraid to say things that might upset the boys. During an interview with Viking FM, Sophia said: 'I think it's a lot easier for the boys to do well because they're five cute boys and the girls are always going to love them and they are really good. I think for us, we just wanted a little bit more help – just because it's harder for us to get people to like us, to get the right song and the right styling.

GIRL GROUP BELLE AMIE WERE VOTED OFF *X FACTOR* IN WEEK FOUR.

'You could put the boys out there in bin bags and sing "Baa Baa Black Sheep" and they'd go through with flying colours. I think it's just a lot easier for them than us.'

Many One Direction fans would have a problem with what Sophia said because the boys needed to work so hard every week to stay in the competition. They had to put in long hours at the studio to make sure their performances were amazing. Maybe One Direction initially had it a bit easier because they were a boy band, but they couldn't afford to be complacent.

While Sophia was living in the house there were rumours that something might be going on between her and Niall, despite Niall being several years younger. Newspapers reported that they had kissed on the lips and kept hugging. Some fans asked Belle Amie what was going on and they set the record straight in their video diary. Sophia revealed: 'I can honestly, openly say that there is nothing going on between me and Niall. Niall is like a little ba–ba to me. He is seven years younger than me, and that would just be weird! As cute as he is, he is still all yours, girls, so don't you worry!

'They are good to have fun with and they always want hugs, but they are literally like our little brothers.'

Geneva added: 'Just like what Sophia said, they're like our little buddies – there's honestly nothing going on. We're focused on the prize. There is honestly nothing going on, they are all yours!'

Meanwhile, the boys loved joking around with the Belle Amie girls and winding them up. When asked what theme the girls would pick for a week if they were given the choice, they said 'moaning' because apparently the girls love to moan. Their room was directly above the girls' and so they would stomp about and try to make as much noise as possible when Belle

Amie were trying to get some sleep. They would also steal their bras and run around with them on their heads. At times, they drove the girls crazy.

When Belle Amie left the competition they didn't hold anything against Zayn, Liam, Louis, Harry, Niall or Simon despite what Louis Walsh said, following their Week Three performance. His comments after they sang 'I'll Stand By You' were: 'I think you're potentially a really, really great girl band but you've got a problem because you're on your own in this competition. Simon Cowell's putting all his energies into the boy band, One Direction – and it's not fair, and that's why he picked that song. It wasn't a great song choice, but what are you to do? You have no mentor!'

Afterwards, Sophia explained to TalkTalk: 'I was a bit embarrassed when Louis said it because you don't know how to react. We started bickering with him onstage. It was just a bit of a shock because we'd never thought of that, but it's not true: Simon gave us just as much attention.'

Zayn told the backstage cameras: 'For Louis to say that was a bit harsh because it looked like we're the bad guys.'

Harry added: 'It seemed like it took a bit of our hard work away.'

Boot Camp

The Boot Camp was held at Wembley Arena over five days in July 2010 to whittle down the 211 acts that had made it so far. Everyone had to be there nice and early on 22 July because there was a lot to fit in. On arrival, the nervous singers were divided into their four categories: Boys, Girls, Over-25s and Groups. Up until that point, none of their first auditions had been aired on TV so no one had any idea what the other singers were like. Also, they didn't know who their biggest rivals would be until they were given their first challenge. For Niall, it was especially nerve wracking as he had to travel all the way from Ireland to be there.

The Boys were told to rehearse Michael Jackson's 'Man In The Mirror', the Girls were given the challenging Beyoncé track, 'If I Were A Boy', the Over-25s were told to practise Lady Gaga's 'Poker Face' and the Groups were given 'Nothing's Gonna Stop Us Now' by Starship.

Simon Cowell told Zayn, Harry, Liam and the rest of the nervous, but excited hopefuls: 'By the end of the day, half of you are going home. Today, you're going to be put in your categories and you're going to sing one song. There are literally no second chances today.'

In forcing everyone to sing the same song Simon and Louis were making things tenser because the singers felt under greater pressure to put their own unique slant on it. It also meant that some of the acts were singing songs that were not in their usual style. Some of the singers who sailed through their first auditions failed to cope under the pressure and didn't sing well at all. Dermot O'Leary was shocked at how some singers who didn't sing in tune would come offstage and tell him confidentially that they'd nailed it and would definitely be going through to the next round. Our favourite boys weren't so big headed, but they still put in great performances and were thrilled when they were told to come back for Day Two.

After celebrating that they had made it through with some of the other contestants, the boys went back to their hotel rooms because they knew that the next day would be even tougher. And they were right: on arriving at Wembley, all the remaining singers were taken to the stage. Simon and Louis revealed that they would now be taught how to dance by the show's choreographer, Brian Friedman.

Friedman told the contestants: 'I don't want you to be scared: what we are going to work on is your stage presence and choreography.'

Simon had been unsure about introducing a dance element to Boot Camp and so no one was to be eliminated if their dancing skills weren't up to scratch. When this was shown on TV, it was the first time that

THE BOYS HAD A TOUGH TIME AT BOOT-CAMP, PARTICULARLY ZAYN WHO SUFFERED FROM STAGE FRIGHT DURING THE RIGOROUS AUDITIONS.

we could see Zayn – but not for the right reasons. Zayn struggled with learning the dance moves and because he'd never really danced before, he didn't want to perform in front of Simon and the millions of people watching at home. He decided to stay backstage and would have got away with it, had Simon not missed him when the Boys' category danced.

Zayn told the backstage camera: 'I seriously don't want to do it because I hate dancing, and I've never done it before and I feel like an idiot on the stage with other people, who are clearly better than me, and I just feel like an idiot – I'm not doing it!

'I just know I'm going to do it wrong because I don't know it. When you've got to perform in front of Simon and professionals that know what they're doing and how to dance, and professional choreographers and stuff, and I just don't know…'

Usually Simon would have had no time for someone who refuses to do something that he's told them to do, but he felt he had to help Zayn. He refused to allow Zayn to make the biggest mistake of his life and leave because he didn't want to dance: Zayn was too talented a singer to let go.

Rather than hold everyone up, Simon told Brian and Louis that he would go and get Zayn while they carried on watching the other categories.

Simon found Zayn and he asked him: 'Zayn, why

aren't you out there? Why aren't you out there? You can't just bottle it, you can't just hide behind here! Zayn, you are ruining this for yourself. I'm trying to help you here. So, if you can't do it now, you're never going to be able to do it, right? Come on, let's go and do it!' Just before Zayn went onstage, Simon told him: 'Don't do that again, get on with it!' They shook hands and as Zayn went up the stairs to the stage, Simon quickly made it back to the judges' table.

Simon could have been mean and made Zayn dance on his own but instead he let Harry and a few of the other boys dance with him. Zayn definitely wasn't the best and Simon admitted that he looked 'uncomfortable', but he was glad that Zayn gave it a go. Afterwards, Zayn just said that he'd have to work on his dancing skills and his confidence levels, but he looked happy anyway. It's just a shame that Zayn, Harry, Liam, Niall and Louis hadn't been made into a band at that stage: the other lads would have helped Zayn to pick up the dance moves and Simon wouldn't have had to do that.

Harry told the backstage cameras: 'As you go through Boot Camp you kind of realise how big the prize is, so being here the last few days has made me realise how much I wanna stay – I really don't want to go home now.'

On the third day the contestants met the third judge, former Pussycat Dolls singer Nicole Scherzinger. She had been drafted in at the last minute to replace Cheryl Cole, who was recovering from malaria. Cheryl caught malaria during a holiday in Tanzania but she had no idea she had contracted the infectious disease until she collapsed during a photo shoot. At first doctors thought that she had just been working too hard but then they realised she had malaria. Thankfully she was diagnosed early because it can be fatal. She had to spend days in hospital and then it took weeks for her to recover. Simon told her not to worry about *The X Factor* until she was completely well again.

NICOLE SCHERZINGER STEPPED IN FOR CHERYL COLE DURING THE *X FACTOR* BOOT CAMP AUDITIONS.

Nicole was so excited to be back because she had helped to put through Harry and a few of the other singers. Now she wanted to help select the right people for the Judges' Houses round. Because both Cheryl and Dannii wouldn't be at Boot Camp, the *X Factor* producers decided to cancel the live element of the boot-camp week. On the official *X Factor*

Twitter, they tweeted: 'Due to the unusual circumstances, we are not inviting an audience to watch the contestants perform at *The X Factor* Boot Camp.' Thousands of fans were gutted as they'd been looking forward to seeing the performances. Even the contestants were a bit unnerved because they enjoyed the support that the crowd had given them during their first auditions: Liam, Harry and Niall in particular had all been boosted by cheers from the audience when they took to the stage, first time around.

After the contestants were given a song on Day One, some of them found it tough because they didn't especially like their number. On Day Three, they had a list of 40 songs to choose from, which turned out to be a harder challenge because they had to pick one that suited them and get on with rehearsing it. Some people couldn't decide which song to go for and kept switching from one to another, wasting time.

One by one, the remaining contestants had to make their way onstage to perform the song they had chosen. Unlike their first auditions where the judges gave them feedback before telling them they were through, they were simply told 'thanks' and then asked to leave the stage, not knowing if they'd done enough.

Liam picked Oasis' 'Stop Crying Your Heart Out' for his solo performance. He told the backstage camera: 'I want to show Simon that I mean business, and that I have what it takes: this is the moment I've been waiting for.'

Nicole and Louis thought that Liam performed the song wonderfully but Simon wasn't so keen as he had been during the first audition. He told the other judges: 'I like him, but I think it was a little bit one-dimensional.' In fact, the standard was so high during the final performances that it was extremely stressful for the contestants as they waited for their turn: no one wanted to mess up or forget their words.

On the fifth and final day of Boot Camp, it was decision time for Simon, Nicole and Louis. Now they had to pick their favourite acts to put through to Judges' Houses. Normally they pick six acts for each category but they decided to put eight acts through in each one because Cheryl and Dannii had missed the first auditions and Boot Camp (they didn't want them to moan that they hadn't had enough acts to choose from). Nicole was a very confident judge and when it came to finalising who should go in what category, she suggested to Simon that the Over-25s became the Over-28s, which meant the talented twentysomethings could be more evenly shared out.

When the 30 remaining boys were called onstage to find out who would be going through to the Judges' Houses, tensions were running high. Everyone wanted to be picked by the judges, but they knew that the standard had been high throughout Boot Camp.

Simon got the ball rolling: 'The first person through to the Judges' Houses is… John Wilding.'

Nicole: 'Nicolo Festa.'

Louis: 'Paije Richardson.'

Simon: 'Aiden Grimshaw.'

Louis: 'Marlon McKenzie.'

Louis: 'Karl Brown.'

Nicole: 'Matt Cardle.'

Simon: 'The final contestant who's made it through is Tom Richards. That's it, guys – I'm really sorry.'

After making his way offstage, a teary Liam admitted to Dermot O'Leary, 'I just don't want to go home, I just don't want to go.'

Poor Harry could hardly speak as he cried into his hat: 'I'm really gutted.' Niall was inconsolable and said it was one of the worst things that he'd ever had to do in his life: 'Standing there, waiting for your name to be called, and then it's not.' Indeed, Niall was so emotional that he hid his head under his sweater and moved away from the camera. He found it just too painful to talk about.

But before they could leave, a member of staff came and called our favourite five lads back. They were asked to wait onstage with Esther Campbell, Rebecca Creighton, Sophia Wardman and Geneva Lane. No one knew what was happening, but they all hoped that they would be

THE *X FACTOR* BOOT CAMP AUDITIONS WERE EMOTIONALLY DRAINING FOR THE BOYS, PARTICULARLY HARRY WHO WAS CLOSE TO TEARS.

given a second chance – and they got their wish. Nicole spoke to the nine nervous singers first. She said: 'Hello, thank you so much for coming back. Judging from some of your faces, this is really hard. We've thought long and hard about it, and we've thought of each of you as individuals and we just feel that you're too talented to let go of. We think it would be a great idea to have two separate groups.'

Simon then hinted that they should form groups and might meet again in the future, before adding: 'We've decided to put you both through. This is a lifeline: you've got to work ten, twelve, fourteen hours a day, every single day, and take this opportunity. You've got a real shot here, guys.'

Up until then, the boys had been thinking that the judges wanted them to re-audition the following year. They had no idea that they were being put through to Judges' Houses.

When Simon suggested the boys become a band they had to say whether or not they wanted to do so. Harry was keen to accept straightaway, but Liam wanted to think about it first: he wasn't sure because he'd always wanted to be a solo artist and he didn't want to do anything that might damage that. He needed to be sure that being in the band was the right thing for him. We are so glad that Liam decided that it was because One Direction would be nothing without him!

Afterwards, Harry summed up how everyone was feeling: '[I went from] the worst feeling in my life to the best.'

The boys loved the moment when all the people who would be coming to the Judges' Houses were put in the same room. Everyone went crazy and Harry gave Aiden the biggest hug!

Shortly after Boot Camp, the judges found out who would be mentoring each category. Unlike previous years when they have sat in the same room to find out, this time they were scattered across the globe: Simon was in London, Louis was in Dublin, Cheryl was in Los Angeles and Dannii was in Australia. They all had to wait for one of the show's producers to ring them. Simon thought that the Girls were the strongest category, with maybe the Boys as the second strongest. He wasn't at all pleased when he found out that Cheryl had the Girls and Dannii had got the Boys. After he received the phone call to tell him that he would be mentoring the Groups, he asked for the producer to repeat what had been said and then sarcastically replied: 'Thank you for repaying all of my hard work on the show this year.' Simon was pleased that Louis got the Over-28s, but then said of the Girls and Boys going to Cheryl and Dannii: 'I can't believe it – they don't turn up on the auditions. Two words: stitch up!'

Simon might have been initially frustrated to get the

Groups but now he has no regrets. He's so glad that he got to mentor One Direction and turn them into *X Factor* finalists!

Even though the boys found out in July that they had made it from Boot Camp to Judges' Houses, they still had a long time to wait until it was shown on TV. The Boot Camp episodes of *The X Factor* didn't air until Saturday, 2 and Sunday, 3 October 2010.

Zayn, Liam, Louis, Harry and Niall's families were so proud of them that they held Boot Camp parties in their honour. The week that the boys appeared on TV, Louis' mum Johannah told her local newspaper, *Doncaster Today*: 'We had a family party to watch the Boot Camp stages of the show on Sunday and we were all so proud of Louis and the boys. He's so excited, he can't quite believe he has made it this far – it's all a bit surreal for him.'

Johannah knew that Louis and the other boys had already made it to the live shows because they filmed the Judges' Houses shows back in August, but she had to keep it a secret.

Boy Bands

In recent years, boy bands have been labelled uncool but the future now looks rosy, thanks to JLS, The Wanted and One Direction!

By taking part in *The X Factor* the boys have had the

opportunity to meet JLS, The Wanted, Westlife and Take That. Louis, Liam, Harry, Zayn and Niall have been able to see first-hand how the other boy bands work and play together.

Shortly before the boys met JLS, Westlife and Take That in Week Six, Liam told the official *X Factor* website: 'It's great to have all the boy bands coming on the show and we have a lot of questions we want to ask them because they are doing what we want to do. We're looking forward to seeing all of them, but Niall is really excited about Westlife!'

In fact, Niall wanted to meet Gary Barlow, too and Louis was looking forward to seeing Robbie Williams.

Our favourite boys might not have entered *The X Factor* as a group, but they have always admired boy bands. If they had to pick a favourite, then Liam and Zayn would go for 'N Sync, Harry would pick Take That and Westlife gets Niall's vote, 'because they're Irish.' Louis doesn't seem to have a favourite but he's a big Robbie Williams fan, so maybe Take That with Robbie.

All the boy bands that have met One Direction so far are full of praise for Liam, Niall, Harry, Zayn and Louis. One day, they might end up fighting them in the charts but for now, they can just be friends. Shane Filan from Westlife told *X* magazine: 'They're the whole package: they're good singers, they're good-looking lads and

THE ONE DIRECTION BOYS HAD THE OPPORTUNITY TO MEET LOADS OF FAMOUS CELEBRITIES DURING THEIR TIME ON *THE X FACTOR*, INCLUDING ROBBIE WILLIAMS AND GARY BARLOW.

they're quite cool. They're like a band full of Justin Biebers and they've got everything the girls will love.'

Aiden Grimshaw and Katie Waissel have joked that there's no place for The Wanted anymore now that there's One Direction, but many fans would disagree because they like both bands.

DID YOU KNOW?

When Westlife were being interviewed behind the scenes, Niall joined them and pretended to be Kian. He said: 'I just think we're the best boy band out there at the moment – apart from One Direction, of course!'

Mark and Shane asked him about his Botox and Niall replied: 'I've been looking a bit shabby for the last twelve years.'

When Kian arrived, Niall directed him to One Direction, which Kian found so funny. All the Westlife boys wanted One Direction to do well in the competition. And they were also fans of their 'Auntie Mary', as they like to call Mary Byrne.

WESTLIFE ARE BIG FANS OF ONE DIRECTION.

C is for...

Celebrity Fans

Zayn, Liam, Harry, Niall and Louis already have dozens of celebrity fans. They impressed virtually every celebrity who visited *The X Factor* live shows, whether they were sitting in the audience or performing on the Sunday result show. They've also made a good impression on the TV and radio presenters who have interviewed them. Lorraine Kelly has been a massive fan of the boys ever since she interviewed them before the live shows kicked off; she thought Harry and Liam in particular were supercute and polite.

'When Love Takes Over' singer Kelly Rowland and *Heroes'* actress Hayden Panettiere enjoyed watching the boys when they came over to England and ever since, they've been big supporters of them. The Saturdays, especially Mollie King, also backed the boys. Back in October 2010, Mollie told *Now Magazine*: 'I love One Direction, I want them to win!'

US singer Alexis Jordan also thinks One Direction are great. Simon invited her to meet the boys and the other *X Factor* contestants, and she was more than impressed. Alexis got to know Simon when she appeared on the

The Saturdays were right behind One Direction from the very start of The *X Factor* auditions.

first series of *America's Got Talent*. One Direction were her favourite act, followed by Cher Lloyd, but she thought the way all the singers managed to perform in front of millions of people without allowing their nerves to get the better of them was brilliant.

Siva, Max, Nathan, Jay and Tom from The Wanted haven't tried to put One Direction down in interviews because they want to be encouraging rather than treat them as their rivals. In an interview with Heart FM in October 2010, Jay said: 'When we arrived, JLS were really gracious and encouraged us to do well and work hard. I think if we did anything less, it would be a bit unfair, so I just wish them good luck because they're just trying to do what we're trying to do.'

Max added: 'I really like them, actually – I think they're one of my favourites on there because they're the whole package.'

In fact, many of the boys' celebrity fans have been offering advice and wishing them well. Mark Feehily from Westlife thinks they have lots of potential. He told Digital Spy: 'They need great songs, but they've got a lot of potential to be successful. There are other pop acts who've come out over the last couple of years who don't look as good and don't sing as well, but they've done well because they've had great music.

'They've got a lot of work to do – just natural band work. It only happens through time. They've been put together, so they've got to learn to get on with each other day to day, learn how to like each other and find their positions within the group, and when all that happens, they can really take off.'

'And the boys have even impressed former *Strictly Come Dancing* judge Arlene Phillips. She told Konnie Huq on *The Xtra Factor*: 'My youngest daughter is in love with One Direction. When I watched them tonight, with Harry and that microphone and that close up, you know he is going to break millions of hearts and why wouldn't you pick up the phone and vote One Direction?' Arlene also made a very good point when she said that people want to listen to Rebecca Ferguson sing, but they want to watch One Direction. The boys were one of only a couple of acts who owned the *X Factor* stage when they were performing each week.

Cher Lloyd

Seventeen-year-old Cher Lloyd was one of the most talented singers in the competition and she bonded with all the boys during their time in the *X Factor* house. Cher could often be found hanging out with Harry or Liam, chilling in the lounge, making something to eat in the kitchen or practising in the music room. Although this was a competition, none of the acts were afraid of letting the others know what

CHER LLOYD IS GREAT FRIENDS WITH ALL THE ONE DIRECTION BOYS.

songs they would be singing in the live shows. Cher was glad that she had the boys to talk to if she was missing home or having a hard time, and the boys could always make her smile.

Because Liam, Harry, Zayn, Niall and Louis are the same age as Cher the press have constantly matched them up and said one or two of them are dating her. This couldn't be further from the truth – they are just good friends. It's thought that Simon asked them to look out for Cher when they first moved in.

In October 2010, various magazines and newspapers claimed that Zayn and Cher had been kissing and were secretly dating but Cher set the record straight in one of her video diaries. She said: 'You asked if I was going out with Zayn… I'm not! He came in this morning in a green all-in-one! A green all-in-one! I don't think so, I really don't think so. Not cool!'

Cher confessed to the *Daily Star*, who it is that she really fancies: "Nathan from The Wanted, what a hottie! He's single and 17, but I forgot to get his number.

'Nathan, if you're reading this, get my number. Just say hello and make my day!'

When Nathan found out, he was quite flattered and told the *Daily Record*: 'Wow, superb! I've only met her once, but yeah, I think she is a really nice girl. Who knows what the future holds?'

A few weeks later, Nathan was performing on the *X Factor* Sunday result show with his bandmates Max, Siva, Jay and Tom. They got to know each other a bit better, even though they were both really busy. Nathan and Cher didn't have time to arrange a date, but as Nathan explained to *New* magazine: 'I think she's a really nice girl. If I had the time, of course I would take her out. Why not? She's a bit of alright.' His band mate Tom added: 'He gets so excited when she's on the telly… when he sees her, he's all like, "Oooh, shhh, shhh! Look, it's Cher…"'

Harry is well known for being a flirt and just likes having fun. The press have also linked him to Cher and a few other girls, but he's still officially single. He likes talking to girls and told the *Mirror* that the other boys in One Direction do, too: 'We're friends with all the girls in the house. I bought Cher a pork pie, but she hasn't eaten it yet – it's still in the fridge.'

Liam is the third member of One Direction rumoured to be dating Cher. Stories suggest that they got close at Boot Camp and had exchanged secret kisses. But there was no truth in the rumours: at Boot Camp, there was no time for anyone to get romantic – everyone was far too busy rehearsing. Liam told *X* magazine what really happened: 'We made friends downstairs in the hotel at Boot Camp and all I said was, "Do you wanna come back to the room?" I know that sounds bad, but I just meant it in a totally innocent hanging out sense.'

Liam's mum was even asked if anything was going on between her son and Cher. She told *New* magazine: 'There's nothing in it. Liam has a connection with Cher because she's a similar age and they're from a similar part of the country. And he gave her a hug when she got through at Boot Camp, which was on film. It got blown out of proportion.'

It's quite cute that Liam's mum defended his honour. The boys don't really listen to what the papers say about them, but it must be hard for their parents when they keep reading lies. It probably didn't help when Simon's confidante Sinitta suggested something was going on between Liam and Cher in *OK!* magazine because she knows both of them quite well: 'Cher's got all the boys in a lather! I thought it was Cher and Liam. I detected a bit of closeness there. I thought Harry liked either Rebecca or Geneva from Belle Amie.

'I was hoping Liam and Cher was true. He's really calm and sweet, a strong silent type and she's quite fiery and feisty. I thought they could calm each other down and excite each other.'

Cheryl Cole

Cheryl didn't get the chance to meet Liam, Harry, Zayn, Louis and Niall until they were preparing for the live shows. She found out then that they were cheeky chappies.

When they were being interviewed by *X* magazine, Louis said: 'Cheryl was flirting with me yesterday. She asked if I wanted to go for a drink after the show, but that wouldn't be very professional.' But Zayn defended Cheryl and added: 'In his dreams!' before Harry, Niall and Liam started to laugh.

One of the vocal coaches witnessed a bit of banter between the boys and Cheryl on another occasion. She told *Buzz* magazine: 'Louis and Niall from the band were sort of chatting Cheryl up the other night, and she started teasing them, asking if they would like her as a mentor instead of Simon.

'She understands best why they would be attractive to teenage girls, and is always flirting with them because she sees what the young girls see in them.'

The boys might be attractive, but they are far too young for Cheryl. Besides, she is too professional to date any *X Factor* contestant, now or in the future.

X Factor judge Cheryl Cole.

D is for...

Dedication

From the day the boys were put together at Boot Camp, they have worked non-stop to get where they are today. In previous years when the judges have formed bands, they were sometimes left feeling disappointed by the band's lack of preparation, even though they'd been given a second chance. But Miss Frank weren't like that in 2009, and One Direction wanted to make sure that they made the live shows, too: all five boys were dedicated to working as a team to turn themselves into the best boy band they could be.

Just a few days after Boot Camp, the boys all travelled

to Harry's house in Holmes Chapel, Cheshire. Thankfully, it was the summer so they didn't have to miss school or college. For a week, they stayed at Harry's house rehearsing, then they went home for a few days (time for their mums to wash their clothes!) and afterwards they went back for more rehearsals. They spent almost three weeks rehearsing, which was great because they got to know each other properly. If they had lived close by they might have just rehearsed in the day and gone home at night, so it actually worked out for the best that they didn't. They got to see the best and worst parts of each other in those three weeks. Poor Harry's mum had her hands full, with so many lads in the house!

Early on, the boys decided to be professional about their rehearsals. They could have messed around all the time but they knew that they only had a few weeks before Judges' Houses and so they set aside rehearsal time each day and stuck to it (Louis must have found it hard not being allowed to joke around). The boys did argue in those few weeks, but that was to be expected: because they had each entered the competition as individuals, they all had set ideas about the type of singer they wanted to be. They had their own musical styles and even after One Direction was formed, they each had different dreams for the band. It was also hard to decide who should sing lead vocals and who would take care of the harmonies. All the boys would have liked to sing the lead vocals, but that wasn't an option: they each tried out and after practising and discussion, they found their places in the overall group.

E is for...

Elton John – Week Six

Week Six was Elton John Week and the nine remaining acts were to sing Elton John songs. Our favourite boys were a bit unsure at the beginning of the week when they found out the theme because they weren't all that familiar with Elton John's back catalogue. Once they listened to a few songs, however, they decided to embrace the challenge and picked 'Something About The Way You Look Tonight'. Liam told the backstage cameras shortly before they went onstage: 'This has easily been our best week yet and we'd like to end it with a great performance tonight.'

WHO SANG WHAT

Aiden Grimshaw – 'Rocket Man'

Matt Cardle – 'Goodbye Yellow Brick Road'

Paije Richardson – 'Crocodile Rock'

Rebecca Ferguson – 'Candle In The Wind'

Katie Waissel – 'Saturday Night's Alright (For Fighting)'

Cher Lloyd – Mash up of 'Sorry Seems To Be The Hardest Word' and Eminem's 'Mockingbird'

Wagner – Mash up of 'I'm Still Standing' and 'Circle Of Life'

Mary Byrne – 'Can You Feel The Love Tonight'

One Direction – 'Something About The Way You Look Tonight'

WHAT THE JUDGES THOUGHT OF ONE DIRECTION'S PERFORMANCE

Louis Walsh: "Well, boys, after that performance I think you're only going in one direction, and that direction is the final. I talked to you guys a lot yesterday and I really got to know you. I know that you're taking the whole thing really, really serious and you know, going to be the next big boy band, and you've gelled as friends and I've nothing but good to say about One Direction!'

Dannii Minogue: 'Guys, you are so consistent, it's

scary! That song could have been really boring, but it was great – that's what I would love to hear you sing at your concerts, which I'm sure you will be doing one day [crowd cheers].

Cheryl Cole: 'Listen to that! That's what it's about; to hear that is the measure of what you've become, so you definitely are heading in one direction.'

Simon Cowell: 'Guys, I want to say something, okay? This is the first time in all the years of *X Factor* where I genuinely believe a group are going to win

MATT CARDLE WAS ONE OF THE MOST POPULAR X FACTOR CONTESTANTS OF ALL TIME.

this competition. And you know what? I want to say this, what was so impressive, you've seen the girls and anything else you've remained focused, you've been really nice to the crew, you're nice to the fans and most importantly, everything that happened tonight from the choice of song to what they wore, it was all down to you. Guys, congratulations!'

THE BOYS MEET AND
GREET FANS AT A FILM
PREMIERE IN LONDON.

WHAT THE BOYS THOUGHT

Louis, Zayn, Liam, Niall and Harry were really pleased with their performance and they were also blown away by the judges' comments. Simon might have said it was all down to them, but they think he plays a big part, too – they loved having him as their mentor. Being out of their comfort zones ended up giving them their best performance to date, which was quite a surprise.

Louis told the official *X Factor* website: 'Last night was absolutely incredible, the crowd were amazing.' Zayn added: 'The competition's really, really heating up.'

THE SING–OFF

Aiden and Katie received the lowest number of votes and so they had to sing for survival. Katie sang 'Save Me From Myself' by Christina Aguilera and Aiden's choice was 'Don't Dream It's Over' by Crowded House. Simon and Cheryl voted to send Aiden home, while Dannii and Louis decided to send Katie home and so it went to the public vote. Aiden received the least amount of votes and so he became the eighth act to leave the show.

F is for...

Fans

From the day Liam, Harry and Niall's first auditions were shown on TV they started having fans. Liam was probably more used to having fans wanting his autograph because he had been on the show before. For Harry and Niall, though, it was the first time. Their first fans even set up fan sites and the first Liam fan site was called www.liampayneonline.com. It has a forum so fans can chat about Liam and it shows his latest Facebook messages and tweets, too. The other guys didn't have their own individual fan sites built.

The first One Direction fan site (www.onedirection fanclub.co.uk) was set up after Judges' Houses by

LIAM SAYS 'HI' TO
FANS OUTSIDE *THE X
FACTOR* TV STUDIOS.

superfan Laura Dack. It's a great site, with an awesome photo gallery that you should check out; it's an excellent place to get to know about the band and it has some cool polls, too. Visitors have voted Harry the fittest member of One Direction with 36 per cent of the votes cast and Liam as the band mate who sings best solo, 38 per cent of the votes cast. Two weeks before *The X Factor* final, it was revealed that 81 per cent of visitors thought that One Direction would win!

There are other fan groups and pages on Facebook that you can join but you are best sticking to the official ones run by the boys themselves. Lots of people seem to be pretending to be them, but the official groups and pages have photos you won't see anywhere else.

The boys enjoy having lots of dedicated fans but it took a while for them to get used to being followed everywhere. On 29 October 2010 one fan did get injured though, which must have been upsetting for the boys. She had been waiting to see them in London and when they arrived by taxi, she somehow managed to get her foot stuck underneath their taxi. Ouch!

What had caused the accident was that the girl and some other fans had run over to the taxi, screaming, and the driver decided it would be best if he pulled away – he wanted to keep the boys safe. In the panic, the taxi's wheel accidentally went over her foot. The girl was rushed to hospital after paramedics put her foot in a foot brace and wheeled her into an ambulance.

Her friend tweeted a few hours later: 'My friend went to The X Factor Studios today and the car that One Direction were in ran over her foot and now she's in hospital.'

Thankfully, nothing like that has happened since but fans should always wait and let the boys leave their vehicles before they approach them.

On another occasion, *X Factor* bosses allegedly had to call in riot police to try and calm down fans who had decided to climb onto a glass roof so that they could see the boys. The *X Factor* crew do have lots of security guards to protect the acts but needed backup to get the fans off the roof. If the roof had given way, the fans could have crashed through and injured both themselves and the boys.

Since then, the One Direction fan base has kept on growing and growing so more fans are turning up to try and catch a glimpse of the boys. They will wait for hours in the freezing cold and snow to see their favourite band for thirty seconds; they are really dedicated.

Sometimes the boys can get in trouble for encouraging fans to come and see them because so many turn up and it's hard for their security team to control them. When JLS, Westlife and Take That were due on the Sunday results show in Week Six, Harry tweeted: 'Can't wait to meet JLS, Westlife and Take That. Everyone should come down on Sunday' and Louis tweeted: 'Sooooo excited to meet Take That, JLS and Westlife, hopefully gonna come out as a group to meet all the fans outside the studio!!' Any fans who lived nearby or could get to the studio made the journey – they didn't want to miss out!

One Direction fans will do anything to get close to their favourite boys or get a wave from them. Some fans climb trees so they can see over the crowds and security barriers, others try to take the security fencing apart – they just get overcome with excitement and then do things that they wouldn't normally do. Liam, Louis, Niall, Harry and Zayn are so impressed by the way that the fans are willing to wait for them, almost twenty-four hours a day. They only have to walk past the security fences and the girls start to scream, even before they see who it is.

But the fans don't just want autographs from the boys: they want to give something back, too. They make them special bracelets, buy teddies, sweets, bake cakes and put together amazing scrapbooks for the boys to keep. When it was snowing, they wrote messages for One Direction in the snow and sent them the photos on Facebook. This year's *X Factor* house wasn't on a regular street, which meant the fans couldn't wait outside. It was a bit of a shame for the

THE BOYS LEAVE *THE X FACTOR* PARTY IN GOOD SPIRITS DESPITE COMING THIRD OVERALL.

HARRY MEETS FANS
OUTSIDE *THE X
FACTOR* STUDIOS.

fans, but at least it allowed the boys to get a good night's sleep! In previous years, the fans had woken up the occupants of the house with their screaming, refusing to give up until they came outside.

Other fans have come up with unique gifts that might seem strange to other people but suit the boys down to the ground. Two fans sent Harry a photo of carrots they had made to look like each member of the band. Harry was impressed and thanked the girls via Twitter. Another fan sent them five mushrooms, which had been customised with eyes and hair so they looked like the boys.

The boys have signed hundreds of autographs in the last few months but they will be signing even more now the show is over. Some fans don't want them to just do their autographs on paper, though: they want them to sign more unique places.

The lads confessed to the *Daily Star*: 'A couple of fans asked us to sign their big toenails. It wasn't that gross, it was OK. I guess there are worse places to sign.'

Fashion

Following fashion and looking good is very important for all pop stars. When people audition for *The X Factor* they have to make sure that they dress to impress. Simon is forever commenting if they look as if they've made no effort. Harry, Liam, Niall, Zayn and Louis had to be sure they picked outfits that showed off their personalities when they auditioned for the first time. Thankfully, they have supportive mums who will have helped them pick the right clothes to wear and made sure those clothes were ironed, too!

Harry wore a white T-shirt, grey cardigan, green and black scarf and casual trousers for his first audition. He looked casual, but smart at the same time. Liam also picked a white T-shirt, but his was tighter than Harry's; he also wore dark blue jeans, big black boots and a black belt. His look was smart and sophisticated. He looked gorgeous! Two years earlier, he had chosen a smart striped shirt with a black waistcoat, jeans and black shoes for his audition. His 2010 outfit showed the judges how much he had changed: he was no longer a little boy. Niall looked very different from Liam and Harry in his audition: he wore a red, green and white checked shirt, with a green T-shirt underneath, jeans and trainers. His look was casual and cheeky!

For the Judges' Houses round, the boys had to combine their fashion styles and come up with one unified look. They all wore grey or white pumps (apart from Louis who had a sore foot and had to wear flip-flops), casual three-quarter length trousers or shorts and loose-fitting shirts or T-shirts. The colours were all blue, white and brown, no one stood out in bright colours:

ZAYN IS ONE OF THE
MOST STYLISH MEMBERS
OF THE BAND.

they still showed their own fashion style, but in a subtle way. Harry still had a scarf on and Niall wore a buttoned-up shirt as he did in his audition.

From Boot Camp, all the contestants got to meet the show's stylists and received advice on what they should wear, but the overall look for Judges' Houses was chosen by Liam, Harry, Louis, Zayn and Niall themselves. When it came to the live shows, the stylists would fill a rack of suitable clothes for each performance and the boys could choose whatever they wanted to wear. If they were going for a smart look, they all picked smart clothes that had some shared elements but weren't identical. Sometimes they would change their minds and would have to pick new outfits just hours before the performance. They were always willing to try something that they wouldn't normally wear to see if it looked good.

During the week, the boys wore their own, more casual clothes. They had long days rehearsing so they had to wear clothes that were comfortable. Like all the other *X Factor* contestants, they had to wash and iron their own clothes, too. They didn't have their mums around to help!

One day, they were given what looked like large babygros. Zayn picked the green one, Niall went for the US flag, Liam decided to have blue, Harry chose white and Louis went for the more traditional grey one with

THE BOYS LINE UP IN
THEIR AMAZING
ONEPIECE JUMPSUITS.

patterns. They were actually OnePiece Norwegian jumpsuits and cost £100 each. The boys loved them because they could zip up the hoods, run around and no one would recognise them. They wore them everywhere, even to the corner shop to buy supplies. Meanwhile, the other contestants weren't sure what to make of them: Cher Lloyd didn't like them, but Paije Richardson is a big fan. He had one for Judges' Houses, so officially started the jumpsuit trend!

Paije wore his jumpsuit to be unique but once Liam, Louis, Zayn, Niall and Harry jumped on the bandwagon, he didn't feel like wearing his much (he thinks the boys just wanted to be Power Rangers). Niall says that his USA flag jumpsuit is his favourite item of clothing.

In October 2010, the boys had the opportunity to design their own T-shirt with Very and picked a black tee, with their autographs in white and a huge 'I' (one in Roman numerals) in silver foil. They loved having the opportunity to do something like this and once they received their first T-shirts, they decided to show their fans straight away. They drew I ❤ U on the back and then Harry, Zayn and Louis headed outside. Because hundreds of girls followed the boys and other *The X Factor* stars all the time, security fences had been placed around the buildings they rehearsed in. Green sheeting covered much of the railings so the fans couldn't really see what was going on. As the boys walked outside, they started calling to the fans on the other side of the fence and Harry even reached down and touched one fan's leg. A few seconds later, she started to scream: 'Harry's just touched my leg!' She couldn't believe it. As they moved to the section of fence not covered by green sheeting, the crowds moved over and the girls started to scream. The boys teased them first before peeling off their new T-shirts and throwing them over the fence. Poor Zayn didn't throw his high enough, so it got struck on the wire at the top until fans pulled it down. At least it didn't rip! The three girls who got the T-shirts couldn't believe their luck.

Out of all of the *X Factor* contestants, the boys think that Rebecca had the best sense of fashion, but she believes they too have great style. All the contestants designed their own T-shirts, but Liam, Harry, Zayn, Niall and Louis produced the best. Cher's was pretty plain, just a white t-shirt with 'SWAG' and her signature on it, and Katie's was just a simple tee with her eyes on it. The T-shirts were available from the Very store and the boys' T-shirt was given five out of five stars from customers who bought it.

Very were the fashion sponsors of *The X Factor* 2010 and so they invited the boys and the rest of the contestants to be guests of honour at their Christmas Catwalk Show in London's West End. They had to walk down the red carpet and have their photos taken by the paparazzi. While the other guests took their seats, Harry and Rebecca had to introduce the show. Naturally, the boys had to make sure that they looked hot and on trend because it was a fashion show. They all wore dark jeans, boots and stylish tops. Zayn had a lovely red knitted jumper on and Louis wore a scarf similar to the one that Harry likes to wear. After the event, they posed for photos with the models and Niall tweeted: 'Very very much like meeting models at the Very show.' At the end of the event, the *X Factor* contestants all left with big goody bags crammed full of lots of free stuff from Very.

On 11 November 2010, someone from the Jack Wills clothing store in Covent Garden tweeted Harry to ask: 'What are the rules on what you wear on the shows? If we gave you a free jw shirt?' Harry replied: 'I can wear it J I'll be coming in tomorrow. see you soon. xxx.'

And yes, Harry received a lovely white shirt with a red logo from the store and was planning to wear it for his Elton John Week performance. During a fashion themed video for the official website, Louis pointed out the shirt and made sure that he namedropped so everyone knew where the shirt was from. Maybe they'll get more free clothes from the store in the future. In the end, however, Harry didn't wear the shirt for the actual performance because *The X Factor* stylists decided that

HARRY LOOKS
SO CUTE IN HIS
BEAR HAT.

they were too dressed up and changed the band's look. The boys weren't the only ones to have a last-minute change of costume, though: Rebecca and Wagner were also given new outfits.

The *X Factor* stylists even pick out the perfect boxers and socks for Harry, Louis, Niall, Liam and Zayn. For American Anthems Week, they were given brightly coloured socks and boxer shorts with stars on them. They did have a say in all this, though, and if they didn't want to wear something, they only had to let people know and their outfits would be changed.

All five bandmates have now become fashion icons and young boys look up to them: they think Zayn, Harry, Louis, Liam and Niall look really cool. And girls like it when they look cute in their jumpsuits, or when Harry wears his bear hat.

Final

The final of *The X Factor* 2010 saw four acts go head to head. One Direction were up against Matt Cardle, Rebecca Ferguson and Cher Lloyd. Former *X Factor* winners Alexandra Burke and Joe McElderry thought that One Direction would win. Diana Vickers and Max George sent them good luck messages on Twitter too.

The days leading up to the final had been jam-packed for Liam, Louis, Harry, Zayn and Niall. They enjoyed a Christmas meal with the rest of the finalists and Konnie Huq, put in extra rehearsals and spent a day travelling all over the country as they visited their respective home towns.

Sadly for Niall, they couldn't fly over to Ireland because of the snow – they might have got stuck over there and have had to miss the final, so instead they headed to a TV studio to do a live link with Ireland AM. They knew that they would make it up to their Irish fans by performing in Ireland one day in the future. Niall and the boys loved having the opportunity to speak to their fans on the big Irish breakfast show and, as soon as they had finished at Granada Studios, they jumped in their car and headed to Louis' old school in Doncaster.

Everyone at Hall Cross School went crazy the second they saw One Direction. There were hundreds of people lined up in the school playground just hoping to catch a glimpse of the boys. They couldn't believe that they had taken the time out to visit their school – and when the band stepped out on the school's stage they were greeted by cheers and chanting. Louis was blown away and found the whole experience more nerve-wracking than stepping onto the *X Factor* stage.

The boys were soon on the road again, this time heading for Harry's home in Holmes Chapel, Cheshire. They were so impressed with the home-made banners people had brought and they enjoyed a small party with Harry's mum and stepdad. After a quick catch-up, they headed to Bradford's HMV store. Zayn was shocked to see hundreds of fans lined up outside. Only a few months earlier he could have walked inside and no one would have batted an eyelid. Louis told the *X Factor* cameras: 'It was like nothing we'd ever seen before.' Zayn admitted that he'd love to do an album signing in the shop one day.

The boys might have been tired but they had one more thing to do. They were due in Wolverhampton to perform in front of thousands of fans. Simon came along and they had an absolutely amazing time. Liam told fans in their video diary: 'Wolverhampton was absolutely awesome, the crowd were absolutely amazing. Five thousand people were there waiting for us and we went on stage and did three songs and it was the best gig any of us had ever done.'

Harry added: 'It's really exciting for us to think we're going to be doing loads of little gigs like that and some to bigger crowds than that.'

Liam finished their last ever *X Factor* video diary by saying: 'We just really want to thank everybody for all the support we've had so far throughout the competition and we just can't believe it, it's unreal. Thank you so much to everybody who's been voting for us and please keep voting.'

It was lovely that the boys spent the day visiting Doncaster, Holmes Chapel, Bradford and Wolverhampton as it would have been easy for them to just pick one home and miss out the others. All the other finalists only had one place to visit so it was a lot easier for them.

SATURDAY – WHO SANG WHAT

Matt Cardle – 'Here With Me' by Dido

Rebecca Ferguson – 'Like A Star' by Corinne Bailey Rae

Cher Lloyd – Mash up of '369' by Cupid ft B.o.B and 'Get Your Freak On' by Missy Elliott

One Direction – 'Your Song' by Elton John

WHAT THE JUDGES THOUGHT OF ONE DIRECTION'S PERFORMANCE

Louis Walsh: 'Hey One Direction you're in the final, I hope you're here tomorrow night. It's amazing how five guys have gelled so well. I know you're all best friends. I've never seen a band cause so much hysteria so early in their career. I definitely think that you've got an amazing future. Niall, everybody in Ireland must vote for Niall, yes!'

Dannii Minogue: 'Guys, you have worked so hard in this competition. You were thrown together, you deserve to be here and I'd love to see you in the final tomorrow.'

Cheryl Cole: 'You know what... I have thoroughly enjoyed watching you guys growing every week, having the most amount of fun possible and I think that you deserve to be standing on that stage tomorrow night.'

Simon Cowell: 'I just would like to say after hearing the first two performances tonight, Matt and Rebecca, they were so good my heart was sinking. And then you came up on stage, you've got to remember that you're sixteen, seventeen years old, and each of you proved that you should be there as individual singers, you gave it 1000%, it's been an absolute pleasure working with you. I really hope people bother to pick up the phone, put you through to tomorrow because you deserve to be there.'

DUETS – WHO SANG WHAT

Matt Cardle – 'Unfaithful' with Rihanna

Rebecca Ferguson – 'Beautiful' with Christina Aguilera

Cher Lloyd – Mash up of 'Where Is The Love' and 'I Gotta Feeling' with Will.i.am

One Direction – 'She's The One' with Robbie Williams

What the Boys Thought

Louis and Liam couldn't believe that they were given the opportunity to sing with Robbie Williams. They are both huge fans and just being on stage with him was a dream come true — it was something they will never forget. As they finished singing all the boys and Robbie had a hug and he even picked Niall up. Robbie told Dermot that he understood how the boys were feeling at the start of their journeys and it was clear from the way Robbie was with the boys that he'll be keeping in touch with them and helping them in whatever way he can.

Harry admitted to Dermot: 'It's just incredible, it's such an honour to sing with Robbie.'
Simon added: 'Robbie is a great friend to the show, very, very generous with his time and he's made these boys... night of their lives. Thank you, Robbie.'

The next day, Niall admitted that it had been one of the best days of his life.

The Result

Cher received the fewest number of votes so she became the thirteenth act to leave *The X Factor* 2010. The remaining three acts would return the next day to see who would be crowned *X Factor* champion 2010. The boys were so happy to get through.

SUNDAY – WHO SANG WHAT

Matt Cardle – Firework' by Katy Perry

One Direction – 'Torn' by Natalie Imbruglia

Rebecca Ferguson – 'Sweet Dreams' by
  Eurythmics

WHAT THE JUDGES THOUGHT OF ONE DIRECTION'S PERFORMANCE

Louis Walsh: 'One Direction, you're in the final, you could be the first band to win *The X Factor*, it's up to the public at home. But... you've got brilliant chemistry, I love the harmonies. I love the song choice and we've got five new popstars!'

Dannii Minogue: 'Guys, you've done all the right things to make your place here in the final. That was a fantastic performance. Whatever happens tonight I'm sure you guys are going to go on and release records and be the next big band.'

Cheryl Cole: 'It's been so lovely to watch you guys from your first audition. To think that was only a few months ago. I really believe that you've got a massive future ahead of you and I wanna say thank you for being such lovely guys to be around. It's been great getting to know you and good luck with the show tonight.'

Simon Cowell: 'Let's be clear. Anyone who comes into this final has got a great chance of bettering their future. But this is a competition and in terms of the competition, in terms of who's worked the hardest, who I think deserves to win based on the future of something we haven't seen before. I would love to hear your names read out at the end of the competition. Because I think you deserve it.'

THE RESULT

When Dermot announced that Matt and Rebecca would be going through to the final stage of the competition and that One Direction had finished in third place, they were gutted. They looked close to tears because they had put everything into their performances and really wanted to win. Dermot asked the boys what their highlight had been. Louis managed to sum up how all the lads were feeling when he said: 'It's been absolutely incredible. For me, the highlight was when we first sang together at the Judges' Houses ... that was unbelievable and you know what, we've done our absolute best, we've worked hard.'

Zayn added: 'We're definitely going to stay together, this isn't the last of One Direction!'

As the boys made their way off stage, they reflected on what could have been but at the same time decided that they were going to enjoy the rest of the night. They listened to Matt and Rebecca sing their songs, and waited along with the rest of the nation to see who would win. It must have been hard not having the opportunity to sing the song they would have released should they have won because they had rehearsed it and really wanted to show their fans. In the future perhaps they will include this track on their first album.

When Dermot announced that Matt was the winner the boys were over the moon for him because they had said from the beginning that, if they didn't win the show, then they wanted Matt to win. As he was performing his single, all the acts rushed on to congratulate him and our favourite boys were the first to get to him. Harry began singing the lyrics to Matt and Niall tried to get the audience to cheer more. Cheeky Niall managed to get hold of Matt's CD and gave it a kiss. It was clear to everyone watching that the boys were happy and wanted to help Matt celebrate.

As soon as they left the stage they began tweeting: 'Congratulations Matt! Please support Matt by buying When We Collide... iTunes.'

A short time later, Konnie Huq revealed on *The Xtra Factor* that Matt had received the most votes in eleven of the weeks/rounds. The only week he didn't come top was week 1 when Mary Byrne came top and he finished in second place. Rebecca had come second the most in the later stages and One Direction had finished in third place most weeks in the later stages. This proved that Matt was the most deserving winner, even though we wanted One Direction to win.

After things had calmed down, the boys were interviewed by various journalists. When Harry was asked about his X Factor highlight he told digital spy: 'When we walked in and saw the studio for the first time. Then when us five stood behind the doors for the first time on the live show, for that first song – for me that was the best moment. That was where we were actually doing it, the real thing, for the first time. That was a big moment.'

The boys felt that getting through to the final was a special moment too. They were so nervous that they were glad that Dermot called their names first. They might not have won *The X Factor* but they are determined to make sure that they make hit singles and albums in the future.

Food

They say that the way to a man's heart is through his stomach and this is certainly true for the One Direction boys – they love food!

Being away from their parents has meant that Harry, Liam, Louis, Niall and Zayn can eat what they want, but they also have to cook their own meals. During their time in *The X Factor*, the boys lived with the other contestants in a house with a huge kitchen that had every gadget they could have asked for. Because they worked such long hours, they didn't always feel like cooking and so they sometimes shared what another contestant was making or even ordered a takeaway. All the contestants ate a lot of fast food, burgers, pizzas and Indian meals while they lived in the house because it was easier. They enjoyed having McDonald's for breakfast, too!

During the daytime when they were rehearsing in the Covent Garden Studios, the boys would nip out quickly and grab something to eat. Sometimes they would go out for meals in the evening, too: they took Zayn out for Eid (the three-day Muslim holiday that marks the end of Ramadan) with Katie and Rebecca. They went to the award-winning Day of the Raj restaurant in Mill Hill and had a great night.

During their time on *The X Factor*, the boys were asked a lot of questions about food. One fan wanted to know if Harry could only eat one vegetable for the rest of his life, what would he pick? He said sweetcorn. They've also been asked if they could be one type of food, what would it be? Harry said sprouts, Zayn picked a Rogan Josh curry and Liam would be a birthday cake.

For Bonfire Night, the boys had some special guests at *The X Factor* house. A group of cooks from Sainsbury's taught Zayn how to make burgers, Harry learned how to make vegetable fritters, Mary made homemade coleslaw and Katie cooked delicious potato wedges. Harry was really funny when he was cooking his fritters because he pretended to be a stroppy chef. Zayn wore a black wig and became a bit of a cooking expert as he showed the cameraman the correct way to crack an egg.

The housemates also enjoyed a curry night together. Instead of ordering takeaway, the cooks came round and taught everyone how to put on an Indian feast. There was so much food that the boys could have fed fifty people! The cooks liked Liam the best – Louis and Zayn were a bit crazy and wouldn't stop messing about.

During the curry night, Zayn, Paije and John Adeleye took part in the Chilli Challenge: they each had to eat four chillies. If they took a gulp of milk, they would be out. None of the boys had problems eating the first chilli, but John struggled with the second, milder one. Paije hated the third hot chilli and after taking a bite, he swallowed it whole! The fourth (and hottest) chilli must have pushed them to the max, but the boys acted cool. After eating all four chillis, no one had been disqualified or had given up. Officially, it was a draw but Zayn should have been the winner because he didn't struggle like the others: he seemed to want the chillies to be hotter. The three lads celebrated their achievement with a wineglass full of milk each.

Zayn then took part in the Brain Freeze challenge with Geneva from Belle Amie and Paije to see how many ice-cream shots they could do before they experienced 'brain freeze'. In her fifteen seconds, Geneva managed two and then Paije did four. Zayne could have beaten him but he started to laugh, so only

THE BOYS LOVE THEIR FOOD!

managed four. Then it was deadlock: who could eat three shot glasses of ice cream the quickest without using their hands? Poor Paije got covered in ice cream, so Zayn managed to sneak ahead and won. Go, Zayn!

Zayn was always up for the food games and on another evening, he took part in the Fruit Challenge for the *X Factor* website. He had to put his hood over his eyes so he couldn't see and then the cook Zoe spoon-fed him different fruits. The aim of the game was for him to guess correctly what she was feeding him. He managed to guess pomegranate, orange, strawberry and a plum but failed to recognise passion fruit and a raspberry. Afterwards, he admitted that he'd never tried a raspberry before. At the end of the challenge, Zayn laughed and told the camera: 'Join in next week, where Zoe will be eating fruit off my naked body!' Zoe laughed and replied: 'In your dreams!'

As their *X Factor* journeys were coming to an end, the One Direction boys were supposed to be having one last cookery lesson with the Sainsbury cooks. The ladies turned up at the *X Factor* house with all the ingredients and equipment for the boys to prepare a Chinese banquet, but they were still at the studio rehearsing. In the end, the ladies cooked the meal for the boys, jumped in the car and went off to find them. The boys were so glad to see them, they were so hungry and the banquet was amazing – there were so many different things to try! They were each given a fortune cookie and when Zayn opened his, he was really surprised by the ironic message inside. It read: 'If you do not change the direction in which you are going, you will end up where you are headed'.

Football

Whether they're playing or watching it, the One Direction boys love football. Harry, Niall, Louis, Liam and Zayn loved messing around with a footy in *The X Factor* house and they even played in the living room, with the couch as goal.

In November 2010, they got the chance to meet Man United star Rio Ferdinand at the launch of his new footwear range in Selfridges. The boys jumped at the chance to attend the VIP party and were thrilled when he came over to talk to them. They also saw JLS, McFly and footballer Jermaine Jenas. Rio told the boys that he was a big fan and asked if they would like to see England play France at Wembley the following week. The boys couldn't believe it!

Before they could accept, though, they had to speak to Simon and find out if it was okay. Because their schedules were so packed, they needed to make sure that they wouldn't be too tired for rehearsals the next

LOUIS PLAYS KEEPIE-UPPIE WHILE TAKING A BREAK FROM *X FACTOR* REHEARSALS.

LOUIS ENJOYS
VISITING WEMBLEY
FOR THE ENGLAND
VS. FRANCE GAME.

day: they had to put their singing first. However, they were given the thumbs up and ended up having one of the best nights of their lives, even though England lost.

Louis told the official *X Factor* site: 'It was amazing! We just lived out every schoolboy's fantasy and chatted to the players as if they were mates!

'We had a laugh with Steven Gerrard – he told us he wants Rebecca to win, but his wife likes us. We also spoke to Peter Crouch and Gareth Barry, and when we left, we were given the actual match balls they played with!

'It was a magical night capped off by going out onto the Wembley pitch when all the fans had gone home. You got a tingle thinking about all the brilliant players that had played there... we asked if we could have a kick-around but they said no!'

In fact, the boys were given free England shirts and got to sit in the best box in the stadium. Niall wanted to apologise to his Irish fans, though. He tweeted: 'Great night tonight at Wembley... not the best result but met most of the players, went on the pitch... got matchballs.

'Sorry Ireland... I wore an English shirt to the game tonight... Got it free and football is football love it... Gonna get my dad t bring Irish 1.'

While they were there, the boys were also interviewed on FA TV and the presenter asked if they'd be wearing their England shirts on Saturday. 'Not a chance!' said Niall. He asked them what team they supported: Niall said he supports Derby, Liam likes Arsenal and the other three like Manchester United. The boys also revealed that Simon isn't a football fan anymore, but he used to support United.

DID YOU KNOW?

Louis is quite a good footballer and played in a Sunday League team. Zayn is the worst in the group at football – sounds like he'll need a few lessons before the Soccer Six tournament in May 2011! All the best boy bands, singers and celebrities take part and no doubt One Direction will be hoping to beat The Wanted and JLS teams!

G is for...

Girlfriends

Louis is the only member of One Direction who has a girlfriend. Liam, Harry, Niall and Zayn are very much single and would date if they had the time, but they're just so busy!

Harry is the flirt of the group and when he was at Boot Camp, *Xtra Factor* host Konnie Huq picked up on his flirty tendencies. She had fun setting up a date backstage for Harry and one of the girl hopefuls, Katie, who had a bit of a crush on him. And so Konnie got a table, some dinner and drinks and invited Harry to come along for a date. Harry presented Katie with a rose and the two of them laughed together. However,

DESPITE BEING THE ONLY MEMBER OF ONE DIRECTION TO HAVE A GIRLFRIEND, LOUIS IS STILL MOBBED BY FANS WHEREVER HE GOES!

when Katie was called on stage to perform, Harry started chatting to another girl and then a few more girls came over and it was revealed that Harry had been flirting with them all. Then Wagner came and carried Harry off! It was a funny video, and Harry was a good sport for taking part.

The boys won't talk about ex-girlfriends but Louis has said he's kissed about twelve girls in his life and Niall says he's kissed twenty. Harry was eleven years old when he had his first kiss, Liam was ten or eleven, Zayn was seventeen and Louis joked that it was the day before he was asked the question but he wouldn't reveal who it was. Zayn's first kiss was funny because the girl he kissed was really tall and he couldn't reach. He ended up finding a brick to stand on, so he could get to her mouth – he thinks it was a bit like the Yellow Pages adverts!

As for chat-up lines, Louis used to like to ask girls 'Will you marry me?' but he doesn't need those lines any more. He's got his lovely girlfriend Hannah, who he has been dating for quite a while. She used to travel down from Doncaster every week with his mum, dad and best friend Stan for *The X Factor* live shows. Zayn's favourite chat-up line is: 'What's happening?' Liam, Niall and Harry don't use chat-up lines.

The press might have said that Cher Lloyd has been dating Liam, Harry and Zayn, but we know there's no truth in their stories. If Zayn could date any of his fellow *X Factor* contestants, he would have picked Rebecca, not Cher. Liam, on the other hand, *would* choose Cher. Niall would date Treyc, Harry would pick Mary and Louis would fight Harry for Mary. If they could date any celebrity on the planet, Zayn would pick Megan Fox and Liam would choose the gorgeous Pixie Lott. And if he had to pick a celebrity to marry, Liam would go for Leona Lewis rather than Pixie, and Niall would marry Cheryl Cole.

Harry loved it when The Saturdays came to one of *The X Factor* live shows because he got the chance to talk to his dream woman, Frankie Sandford. He was overwhelmed when talking to her and revealed afterwards that he really likes girls with short hair like Frankie's. Harry didn't flirt as much as he usually does with girls he fancies, but he probably will the next time he sees her because he'll be more confident. Frankie's found out that Harry fancies her, but she feels that the age gap of five years is too big. She thinks all the members of One Direction are cute but she wants to look after them, not date them. However, she admitted that she likes Harry's curly hair.

If you fancy one or all of the boys you might want to know what they look for in a girl. Liam likes girls who have nice eyes (he really likes girls with blue eyes in particular). Louis loves messing around and so when he was asked what he looks for in a girl during a video diary, he said: 'I like girls who eat carrots.' Since then, a lot of girls have been sending him carrots, so he's started saying he likes girls with Lamborghinis in the hope that he gets sent one. Harry likes girls who have pretty faces, which made the other lads laugh because they think that's an obvious thing to say. Niall likes cute girls, who have a nice personality and Zayn likes girls who have amazing smiles.

Cher would advise fans who fancy the boys to play it cool. She told *X* magazine: 'The thing you need to do as a girl is try and look like you ain't bothered. That's sort of what I do, like, "whatever, yeah he's hot, not bothered." Brush it off. If you come across as if you really fancy them you're going to scare them off, so hold back a little bit.'

One fan saw the boys outside Subway and tried to put her iPhone in Harry's pocket. Liam thought this was a clever tactic because if she had succeeded then Harry would have had to see her again to return the phone.

Back in November 2010, one newspaper ran a story claiming that Liam had banned Zayn, Niall and Harry from dating during *The X Factor*. It was totally made up as Louis explained to *X Magazine*: 'Absolute tosh, the entire thing! Liam wouldn't be able to slap a girl ban on us, if he tried.'

He added: 'This is the first I've heard of it. Am I

supposed to have slapped a girl ban on myself, too? That would just be stupid.'

It wouldn't be fair even if he had because Louis was allowed to have a girlfriend. All the guys are pretty romantic, though. Liam would like to whisk a girl off on a romantic holiday and Harry would write them a song. Their top three romantic songs are 'Make You Feel My Love' by Adele, Lemar's 'The Way Love Goes' and 'I Don't Wanna Miss a Thing' by Aerosmith.

A FAN IS DELIGHTED AFTER HER FAVOURITE MEMBER OF THE BAND SIGNS HER FOREHEAD!

Guilty Pleasures – Week Three

For the third show, the twelve remaining acts had to sing songs that were their guilty pleasure. Originally, the boys had planned to sing another song but Simon advised them to change it with only a day to go.

WHO SANG WHAT

Aiden Grimshaw – 'Diamonds Are Forever' by Shirley Bassey

Matt Cardle – '...Baby One More Time' by Britney Spears

Paije Richardson – 'Ain't Nobody' by Chaka Khan

Rebecca Ferguson – 'Why Don't You Do Right' by Nora Lee King

Treyc Cohen – 'Whole Lotta Love' by Led Zeppelin

Katie Waissel – 'I Wanna Be Like You' from Disney's *The Jungle Book*

Cher Lloyd – Mash up of 'No Diggity' by Blackstreet and Tears for Fears' 'Shout'

Mary Byrne – 'I Who Have Nothing' by Shirley Bassey

Wagner – Mash up of 'Spice Up Your Life' by Spice Girls and Ricky Martin's 'Livin' La Vida Loca'

John Adeleye – 'Zoom' by Fat Larry's Band

Belle Amie – 'I'll Stand By You' by The Pretenders

One Direction – 'Nobody Knows' by Pink!

WHAT THE JUDGES THOUGHT

Louis Walsh: 'You just have to walk out on the stage: everybody's screaming, it's like five Justin Biebers! And Liam, brilliant lead vocal from you! This band, you're really getting your act together. I think you are the next big pop band.'

Dannii Minogue: 'Being a band, everybody wants to live that dream with you. And it seems like you're living the dream, and loving the dream, and you're letting everyone in on that with you. Another great performance! I'm not sure why Pink is a guilty pleasure, though.'

Cheryl Cole: 'You know what, guys? Let me just put this out there: you are *my* guilty pleasure! When you watch the VT and you see all the hysteria you caused when you went out there this week, that's what you should do. That's what boy bands should be about. Whenever The Beatles went anywhere, they caused that level of hysteria. You're finding your feet now, I'm looking forward to seeing you improve even more.'

Simon Cowell: 'With regards to the song, we chose a song, didn't work. But the good thing about you guys is that there's no bleating on about excuses. "I can't do this", "I can't do that"… It's just a song, you grabbed hold of it within 24 hours, practised. And I've got to tell you, apart from it being a great performance, I thought vocally, you've really, really made some really huge improvements. It's been an absolute pleasure working with you lot.'

WHAT THEY THOUGHT

Harry told the backstage cameras: 'The comments were absolutely brilliant. For us to keep proceeding in the competition, we have to get better every week.'

Zayn admitted that changing the song at the last minute had been stressful but that they agreed with Simon. Liam thought the new song was better because it was a ballad and Dannii had wanted them to sing something slower; it showed everyone that they can perform all sorts of songs well.

The boys have also revealed what their top three 'guilty pleasure' tracks are. In first place, it has to be John Travolta singing 'Greased Lightning', second comes 'Tease Me' by Chaka Demus & Pliers and in third is 'I'm Too Sexy' by Right Said Fred.

H is for...

Hair

If you ask any One Direction fan to describe three things they love about the boys, they would say: their voices, their looks and their hair. Everyone loves Harry's, Liam's, Louis', Niall's and Zayn's hair!

Royston Blythe, Liam's hairdresser back home in Wolverhampton, is such a big fan that he decorated his salon window with posters of Liam and One Direction. Liam has been a client of his for years (his favourite stylist is Ashley Gamble) and when he had some time off between *X Factor* live shows, he popped in to see the staff there. But Liam isn't their first famous client: Katie Price, Lily Cole and Hollywood actor Mickey Rourke

ADAM REED,
MADONNA'S HAIR-
STYLIST, NOW LOOKS
AFTER HARRY'S
CURLY LOCKS.

have all had their hair cut by Royston and his team. Royston got all his staff to vote for One Direction and encouraged the clients to back them, too. He thinks Liam is an amazing person after he sang for free during an event at the salon to raise money for local charities.

Royston told the *Birmingham Mail*: 'He's a very professional person, he's a very well-mannered young man and that's an added bonus because he's a great singer as well. Even from the age of fifteen, he had a great voice. When he came to the shop, he was such a nice lad and when we first heard him sing, we just knew he'd got it. We just knew he was going to get bigger and bigger.

'He was always a pin-up, even before he went on the show. All our juniors like him.'

Liam's mum Karen and his sisters, Ruth and Nicola, all have their hair cut at the same salon, so Royston is always kept up to date with what's going on with Liam and the band.

When Liam made it to the live shows, he was given an awful cut by the *X Factor* hairstylists. All the singers got a makeover that was supposed to make them look better, but Liam looked worse!

Some people in the media and on Twitter started saying Liam had 'Lego helmet' hair. Poor Liam must have been devastated because he has always taken pride in his appearance and liked his old style.

Thankfully, he was allowed to change it back and he posted a photo on Twitter with the message: 'Hair been redone much happier.'

Liam knows he can now pop home and have his hair done by his usual hairdresser any time he wants a cut. During *The X Factor* live shows, all the acts had to visit a hairdressing room so that the stylists could do their hair on Saturdays and Sundays. On the wall was a poster of Harry with hair stuck all over it – yuck! A 'Dirty Harry' headline was stuck on the mirror, too.

Adam Reed, the show's hairdresser, gave Zayn the hairstyle of a 'model of the moment' and he let Harry keep his curly locks. Reed is Madonna's hairdresser and he has also worked for Lady Gaga. Harry's sister Gemma used to be his hairdresser, but *The X Factor* banned her from cutting his hair again as soon as he made the live shows. Since Adam has been looking after Harry's hair, it has been in much better condition because Harry only washes it once a week. Adam advised him to do so because the natural oils in the hair start to work. He uses dry shampoo as well as normal shampoo on Harry's hair.

As well as having their hair done in the hairdressing room, the boys also have make-up applied to their faces for the live shows, which must be a bit weird. To make their skin feel soft and refreshed, they have to put all sorts of creams and lotions on their face every day; they even have eyebrow gel smeared on their eyebrows and lip balm on their lips. Harry likes to joke that Zayn wears make-up all the time; he also likes getting his make-up done by a stylist called Christina because she's good-looking!

'Halloween' – Week Four

The final eleven acts had to sing a song with a Halloween theme in Week Four. This was a night full of witches, zombies and vampires as all the acts wore scary costumes.

WHO SANG WHAT

Aiden Grimshaw – 'Thriller' by Michael Jackson

Matt Cardle – 'Bleeding Love' by Leona Lewis

Paije Richardson – 'Back to Black' by Amy Winehouse

Rebecca Ferguson – 'Wicked Game' by Chris Isaak

Katie Waissel – 'Bewitched' by Steve Lawrence

Cher Lloyd – 'Stay' by Shakespears Sister

Treyc Cohen – 'Relight My Fire' by Take That

Wagner – 'O Fortuna/Bat Out Of Hell' by Meatloaf

Mary Byrne – 'Could It Be Magic' by Barry Manilow

Belle Amie – 'Venus' by Bananarama

One Direction – 'Total Eclipse Of The Heart' by Bonnie Tyler

WHAT THE JUDGES THOUGHT

Louis Walsh: 'First, I was thinking why were you picking this song? But it absolutely worked. I love the whole *Twilight*, vampire thing going in the background, and you definitely gel as a band. Everywhere I go, girls are saying, "You know One Direction, tell One Direction, I love them." I think there's definitely something great about you; you definitely gel as friends. I love the way you all sing. Simon, it's definitely working. I'm not sure what the song's got to do with Halloween but guys, you're brilliant, keep doing it!'

Dannii Minogue: 'Guys, like I've said before you are a boy band doing exactly what a boy band should do. I'm looking at you and thinking the styling is even better than any other week. You make vampire hot, I want to come to your party!'

Cheryl Cole: 'It doesn't matter where I go, somebody, an older woman, young women, kids… everybody mentions One Direction. I think you have a really long way to go in this competition.'

Above: The boys say 'hi' to their fans whilst out and about in London.

Below left: Niall pens a quick 'ditty' in between *X Factor* auditions.

Below right: Harry arrives at the TV Studios on the eve of another *X Factor* showdown.

Left: *X Factor* judge Simon Cowell was One Direction's mentor on the show and his guidance is a big part of their success.

Right: Dannii Minogue was also a massive fan of the boys and championed them from the start.

Above: Niall, Louis and Liam pose for a photo prior to arriving for a rehearsal.

Below: The boys take a night off and head to Wembley for an England game.

Simon Cowell: 'Once again, a great performance. What I really admire about you guys is I know people are under pressure when you go into a competition like this, you've got to remember you're sixteen, seventeen years old, the way that you've conducted yourselves: don't believe the hype, work hard, rehearse. Honestly, it's a total pleasure working with you lot.'

WHAT THE BOYS THOUGHT

Harry told the backstage cameras the next day: 'Last night felt brilliant. We got a real chance to show off our vocals and hopefully the fans at home will vote and keep us in because we really don't want to go home now.'

And their fans did vote and they sailed through to the next round. The boys were really grateful to Simon for picking such a great classic song for them to sing because they felt that everyone at home would know it. A few of the songs they had sung earlier in the competition, they felt, were less well known.

THE SING–OFF

Belle Amie and Katie received the lowest number of votes and so they had to sing for survival. Katie sang 'Trust In Me' by Etta James and Belle Amie chose Kelly Clarkson's 'Breakaway'. Simon and Louis voted to send Katie home, while Dannii and Cheryl wanted

KATIE WAISSEL WAS ONE OF THE TRUE SURVIVORS OF SERIES SEVEN OF *THE X FACTOR*, EVENTUALLY LEAVING THE SHOW IN WEEK EIGHT.

to send Belle Amie home and so it went to deadlock. Belle Amie received the fewest votes from the public and became the sixth act to leave the show.

Harry Styles

Harry is one of the most popular members of One Direction. Born on 1 February 1994, he is from Holmes Chapel in Cheshire. He is the youngest member of One Direction. His middle name is Edward and his nickname at home is 'H'.

Harry's family lived in Evesham when he was born but they moved to Holmes Chapel when he was still a baby. He is really close to his big sister Gemma and they don't argue all that much, but when he puts on silly voices it winds her up. Harry's mum and dad are originally from the South so that might explain why Harry doesn't speak with a Northern accent. Harry has a cat called Dusty – he likes cats a lot.

Gemma is currently studying at Sheffield University.

She is really proud of Harry, but she misses him a lot. In fact, she saw more of him while he was doing *The X Factor* than she might have done had he been at college in Holmes Chapel because she travelled down to London every weekend to see him. Gemma was given a special wristband each week to make sure she got into the show and for a while she tried to keep them all on, but she had to take them off after several weeks as she was running out of arm! She kept the Week One wristband on, though.

Harry's mum is even prouder than Gemma, if that's possible. She told the *Crewe Chronicle*: 'I fill up with pride every time he's on TV. I feel incredibly proud and it's all so surreal to see my boy on the stage. At the end of the day, he's my little baby and there he is on stage in front of millions of people.'

Gemma has only told her friends at Uni that Harry's her brother – she doesn't tell everyone she meets. She rarely gets recognised, but once when she was going into *The X Factor* studios with her family, one of the fans waiting nearby shouted: 'It's Gemma Styles!' That was strange, but nice at the same time.

Harry is a straight-A student and did really well in his GCSEs. His family say he's really talented at everything he tries. Gemma says he's forever picking up new things and becoming good at them, sports such as cricket, football and badminton in particular. Harry proved how good he is at everything when the One Direction boys went bowling. He was the clear winner with 80 points. Second place went to Louis, who scored 59, Liam came third with 52, Niall was fourth with 49, while poor Zayn was in last place with 42. Harry's score was nearly double Zayn's!

Harry had never danced before *The X Factor*, so the whole family were impressed when they saw the dance challenge at Boot Camp. He wasn't one of the main ones featured, but they could make him out in the purple sweater next to Zayn.

Everyone is always asking Gemma what Harry's lovely hair smells like, but she doesn't know – she has never had the urge to sniff it! Gemma thinks it's strange that she has the straightest hair in the world and Harry's is the curliest. Their mum has wavy hair and their dad has really short hair, so no one knows where Harry's curly hair comes from. Apart from their hair, Gemma and Harry look very similar.

Before entering *The X Factor*, Harry had a Facebook account but he had to delete it once his auditions were shown on TV because no one was allowed to know how far he had got in the competition and his friends kept writing congratulations on his wall. *X Factor* bosses could have taken him off, had they found out. Contestants are not supposed to tell anyone, but it would have been pretty obvious to his friends in the summer because Zayn, Louis, Niall and Liam stayed at his house for several weeks. He also went over to Ireland with Niall for Rebecca from Belle Amie's twenty-first birthday party. In the end, it was just simpler to delete his Facebook account and not have to worry about it. There is someone pretending to be Harry on Facebook, however, but it's just an imposter.

At primary school, Harry started singing in shows but then he didn't really do anything in high school. He told the *X Factor* backstage cameras: 'The first time I sang properly was in a school production – the rush that I got was something that I really enjoyed and wanted to do more of.'

Harry only started singing about two years before he auditioned for *The X Factor*. No one in his family is musical, so Harry is the odd one out. He can play guitar and drums a bit, but he's never had lessons.

Before entering *The X Factor*, Harry planned on going to college like his mates and doing A-levels in Law, Sociology and Business. He actually told Simon, Louis and Nicole Scherzinger his plans in his first audition and Simon was impressed. Harry had actually been working in a bakery on a Saturday, but he had to give that up once he progressed in the competition. If Harry hadn't found success as a singer, most probably he would have become a lawyer or a physiotherapist.

During his time on *The X Factor*, Holmes Chapel supported him every step of the way. No one seems to mind what he said about the place in his first *X Factor* video either: 'It's quite boring, nothing much happens there – it's quite picturesque.' Shops and houses had 'Go Harry' and 'Vote One Direction' posters in their windows. The bakery where he used to work even had One Direction loaves on display! Fans love the fact that he used to work in a bakery and a Facebook page called 'Harry Styles works in a bakery. I would check out his buns every day' was set up and has thousands of members.

Harry's favourite song is 'Free Fallin' by John Mayer and he would love to perform with Michael Bublé.

FIVE FASCINATING FACTS ABOUT HARRY

He snores, which must have annoyed the other boys in One Direction when they were sharing a room. His other bad habit is that he can't stop messing with his hair

Harry loves his food and once went to TGI Fridays with his family and ate far too much. On the way home, he threw up all over his sister Gemma

When Harry was little, his mum used to let

him draw on his toast with food colouring before he ate it. He was quite artistic!

He really missed his comfy bed from home when he was living in *The X Factor* house – it was a big change for him, having to sleep in bunk beds

He can juggle!

Help For Heroes

When the boys were invited to take part in a charity single for Help for Heroes, they jumped at the chance. They knew that the money raised would go towards new recovery centres for injured soldiers and they just wanted to help in whatever way they could. Zayn, Liam, Louis, Harry and Niall visited Headley Court Military Rehabilitation Centre on 17 November to meet some of the recovering soldiers and understand a bit more about what they go through once they return to the UK.

The song chosen for the 2010 *X Factor* contestants to sing was David Bowie's 'Heroes'. It was first released in 1977 and over the years, has become the second most-covered Bowie song. Oasis, Bon Jovi, Nicole Kidman and Ewan McGregor have all done covers of the track. All sixteen *X Factor* finalists took part in *The X Factor* 2010 version.

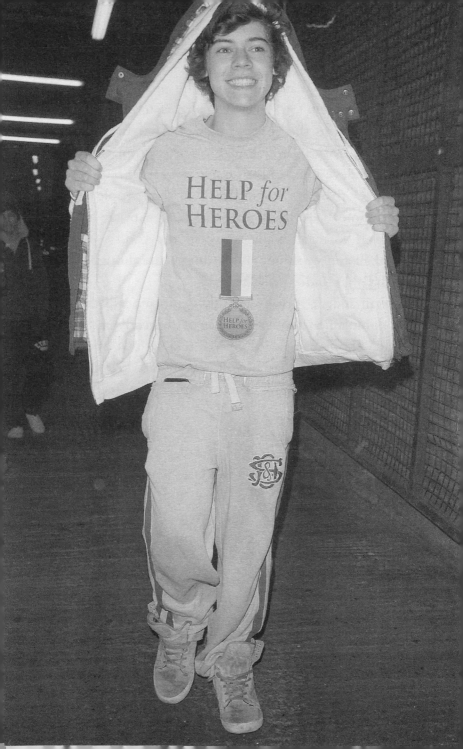

On the day that they filmed the promotional video, staff from Help for Heroes came to watch and answered any questions the contestants had. After hearing some of their stories, Liam told a reporter from the *Sun*: 'I can't believe some of the people who fight out there are younger than me. It's so shocking that people our age can come back from places like Afghanistan disabled forever. We're all really active in the band – we play football and work out all the time – the thought of not being able to do that is horrible.'

Niall added: 'It really puts things into perspective. We all complained about having to get up early and do this video shoot this morning – I feel so bad about that now. You don't realise how lucky you are. We're doing a huge TV show and other people have really, really tough jobs.'

The *Mirror* alleged that during filming Harry and Wagner had to be dragged apart by *X Factor* staff after Harry jokingly rugby-tackled Wagner and then started to play-fight him. They then said that Wagner squared up to Harry and warned him off because he's an expert in karate and could do Harry some serious damage.

The boys all enjoyed making the video because they had never made one before and they were excited about it going on the MTV music channels afterwards. They loved performing the track on *The X Factor* live show a few days later and were thrilled when it went straight to Number 1 in the UK and Ireland. Zayn told Radio 1 host Reggie Yates: 'It was pretty crazy when we were told we got to Number 1 because it's for such a good cause and something we're all really proud about, that makes it so much better.'

In the future the boys might volunteer to record more charity singles for Children in Need or Red Nose Day. They have so many fans that any single they release in the future could raise thousands of pounds for worthy causes.

'Heroes' – Week Two

The remaining 14 acts had to sing songs from their musical heroes in Week Two. One Direction picked a Kelly Clarkson song, which many people thought was an odd choice but considering she won *American Idol*, this was a clever song to go for.

But their sound check didn't go to plan at all: when it came to Harry's turn to sing, he just couldn't. He felt as if he was going to throw up and was rushed to the doctor's. In fact, this turned out to be a bad case of stage fright. No one could blame him for being nervous because it was only Week Two, but for a while it looked as if he wouldn't be able to perform on the live show. Thankfully, he managed to control his nerves and although he didn't feel 100 per cent, he still managed to put in a great performance.

WHO SANG WHAT

Aiden Grimshaw – 'Jealous Guy' by John Lennon

Matt Cardle – 'Just The Way You Are' by Bruno Mars

Paije Richardson – 'If I Ain't Got You' by Alicia Keys

Treyc Cohen – 'Purple Rain' by Prince

Rebecca Ferguson – 'Feeling Good' by Nina Simone

Katie Waissel – 'I Would Rather Go Blind' by Etta James

Cher Lloyd – 'Hard Knock Life' by Jay-Z

Storm Lee – 'Born To Run' by Bruce Springsteen

Mary Byrne – 'You Don't Have To Say You Love Me' by Dusty Springfield

John Adeleye – 'Song For You' by Donny Hathaway

Wagner – 'Just Help Yourself' by Tom Jones

Belle Amie – 'You Really Got Me' by The Kinks

Diva Fever – 'Duck Sauce' by Barbra Streisand

One Direction – 'My Life Would Suck Without You' by Kelly Clarkson

WHAT THE JUDGES THOUGHT

Louis Walsh: 'Well, One Direction, you seem to be having fun on stage. I like the fact that you've gelled already. Every schoolgirl up and down the country is gonna love this. My only problem, boys, is with your mentor, Simon. Kelly Clarkson a hero? Simon, why? It was a strange song. Boys, you are really, really good but I think Simon Cowell could've picked a better song.'

ONE OF THE MOST POPULAR ACTS OF THE EARLY STAGES OF THE COMPETITION, DIVA FEVER, WERE VOTED OUT IN WEEK TWO.

Dannii Minogue: 'Boys, maybe that's your musical hero. I have to say that you're five heartthrobs. You look great together and Harry, whatever nerves you have, I'm sure that your friends and you will stick together. The true measure of a boy band like you will be when you sing your big ballad, so I will be looking forward to hearing that.'

Cheryl Cole: 'I can't even cope with how cute you are – seriously, I can't. I just want to go over and hug them, in a nice way. You're so sweet, I'm watching you the whole time just thinking, "This is adorable". But I want to be able to say, "Wow, this is the new big boy band!" and I think that'll come in time.'

Simon Cowell: 'Okay, well, that time has just come. Let me tell you, you are the most exciting pop band in the country today. I'm being serious – there is something absolutely right.'

WHAT THE BOYS THOUGHT

Niall: 'I think our performance went well last night. We had a good song, the crowd got behind us.'

The boys were so happy that Harry managed to sing with them and they knew his nerves would calm down after a few more performances. They were also pleased when Dermot O'Leary announced that they had got through because they really weren't sure that they would.

STORM LEE BECAME THE THIRD ACT TO LEAVE *THE X FACTOR*, IN WEEK TWO OF THE COMPETITION.

THE SING-OFF

That week, two acts were eliminated. Storm Lee, the act with the lowest votes, automatically left the show. The acts with the second- and third-lowest votes had to face the sing-off. Belle Amie sang 'Big Girls Don't Cry' by Fergie and Diva Fever chose Gloria Gaynor's 'I Will Survive'. Louis, Dannii and Cheryl all voted to send

home Diva Fever, so Simon didn't have to cast his vote.

Storm Lee became the third act and Diva Fever was the fourth act to leave the series.

Home

Home for Harry might have been Holmes Chapel, Bradford for Zayn, Doncaster for Louis, Mullingar for Niall and Wolverhampton for Liam but ever since they made *The X Factor* live shows, London has become the boys' home. They all moved into *The X Factor* house with the other fifteen acts shortly before the first live show on 9 October 2010. Once *The X Factor* finished, they couldn't just go back home: they had to get a record deal, look to move into a new place together and start to decide what sort of music they wanted to record. London will be their new home: it's the place to be for all big music artists because this is where the recording studios, TV studios and big radio stations are located.

The first night that they moved into *The X Factor* house, the contestants all sat round together and had a sing song. Matt Cardle played guitar and everyone had a really great time. That first week was a happy time for them all because the live shows hadn't started and so no one had to leave. As the weeks went by, however, it became more difficult because on a Sunday night the losing singer had to come back, pack their bags and go.

Speaking on GMTV, from his first-ever press conference, Harry admitted: 'The house is always pretty loud. You have your messy people and your tidy people, but it's really good living with all the boys. I miss my mum a little bit, though.'

A few weeks after they moved into *The X Factor* house, Louis told the backstage cameras: 'Living in the contestants' house, it's good to be in a group 'cos if we ever have any problems or on the flip side, if we're up for a laugh then I've got four other lads to turn to, so it's great.

'We all stay in the same room: it's pretty much what you'd expect five teenage lads – it's an absolute tip most of the time.'

In fact, Louis is the messiest member of the group by far.

The boys had their own bathroom in *The X Factor* house so they didn't have to share with the girls, but it really was a pigsty, with lots of boxer shorts everywhere and a carton of orange on the side of the bath!

Liam might be a bit serious sometimes, but he still had an absolute blast every night when they came back from rehearsing. He explained to the *Shropshire Star*: 'It's different. If you don't get to see it and experience it first-hand, you wouldn't understand what it's like. It's so much fun. There is never a dull moment, and it is always loud in the house. That's usually probably coming from our band. Everyone has such a great time and it is surprising how well everybody gets on because at the end of the day, it is a competition but everybody gets on great.'

Things did quieten down as the weeks went by, though. Once people left, their rooms became available and Liam decided to move into a room of his own. He didn't fall out with the boys or anything, he just fancied a bit of space. It made sense really because there were so many free rooms, they could have had one each. Zayn decided to join him and their room was a lot tidier than Louis, Niall and Harry's room. In two years' time Liam would like to have a house in London with One Direction and one in America, too.

In *The X Factor* house, the boys' favourite room was the beanbag room. It had an L-shaped couch, loads of beanbags, a big TV, a table tennis table and a Wii. They also liked the music room, which had a big piano and a jukebox for when they wanted to practise.

I is for...

Illnesses

No one wanted to get ill while they were taking part in *The X Factor* live shows but it was inevitable. Cher, Niall, Rebecca, Paije and Matt all had throat problems, Mary had laryngitis, Harry and Storm caught a bug … there weren't many people who survived all their weeks without a sniffle or two.

Sinitta was really worried for our favourite boy band one week when both Niall and Harry were feeling under the weather. She tweeted: 'Saw XF kids today, poor little Niall from 1 direction has a bad throat so was sent to doctor and Harry threw up again, I think may have a bug.

LOUIS AND HARRY
WRAP UP WARM
ON THEIR WAY
TO *X Factor*
REHEARSALS.

'Please put up some prayers for the wee ones, it's bad enough without getting struck down, mind you Mary recovered in time, I hope they will.'

Rebecca was ill that week, too and she told the official *X Factor* website: 'We're all dropping like flies! Storm and Harry are seeking medical advice so we're all really worried about them.'

All the contestants were ordered to wrap up warm and have plenty of hot drinks. Being rundown can make you more prone to being ill so they tried to rest as much as possible, but it was hard because they had so much to do before the live shows.

But the boys did recover and performed alongside Liam, Louis and Zayn that Saturday. It would take something pretty serious to stop one of them performing – Louis would probably demand to be wheeled on stage on his sick bed if he was ever really ill.

Out of all the band mates, Harry was ill the most during *The X Factor* live shows: he had problems controlling his nerves, stomach bugs, food poisoning and throat problems. Speaking to the official *X Magazine*, Niall confessed: 'The other night we'd got some food in but Harry felt a bit sick. He ran into the toilet but I was doing a poo at the time. He's shouting at me "Get out the way, get out the way!" but I can't move because I'm on the loo. He ends up being sick into the bath. It turned out he burst blood vessels in his neck and he had to go to the doctor. He'd got food poisoning.'

It's funny how the boys are willing to share anything and everything with their fans. Not many pop stars talk about being on the toilet!

Inspiration

Everyone has someone who has inspired them for one reason or another and there are three people who can be described as Harry's musical inspiration: Freddie Mercury, Elvis Presley and Michael Jackson. All these men transformed the music scene and Harry would love to write and perform a track one day that's as good as any of theirs.

Usher is Liam's inspiration: he thinks he's immensely talented and has achieved a lot during his music career. He would like to have the opportunity to interview the five-times Grammy winner one day. Niall says he wouldn't have taken up singing if it wasn't for Frank Sinatra and Michael Bublé. One day he'd love to duet with Michael Bublé or Justin Bieber. Zayn would like to record something with Justin Timberlake in the future.

As they have been growing up, the One Direction boys have also been inspired by their parents and

USHER IS AMONGST ONE OF ONE DIRECTION'S MANY INSPIRATIONS.

grandparents: they all come from families who have supported their musical aspirations and encouraged them to enter *The X Factor*. Everyone remembers the T-shirts that Harry's family wore to his first audition. All five lads are so down-to-earth and genuine because they were brought up in loving homes.

The boys might not recognise it but they have inspired other people to try out for *The X Factor*. Liam in particular is proof indeed even if you get knocked back one year, you can still return to give it another go. It would have been easy for him to give up when Simon said no the first time but because he was determined to prove that he had what it takes, he made it into One Direction and became an *X Factor* finalist!

J is for...

Jealousy

Liam, Louis, Zayn, Harry and Niall are great friends but sometimes they have little arguments. Something would be wrong if they didn't because they're in each other's pockets 24/7. They are never jealous of each other though, whatever the press might say.

Some magazines have claimed that Zayn, Niall and Louis are jealous of Harry and Liam because the press tend to focus more on them in interviews and in the stories they write. This simply isn't true. In the beginning, journalists did want to talk to Liam more because he was on the show before and Harry too because he was the youngest. It's worth remembering that only Liam and Harry's first auditions were shown on the main *X Factor* show so that's why the press focused on them, too. Since the live shows, the press have treated them all pretty equally, however.

Each of the boys has huge armies of supporters who love them individually so it's not like Zayn, Louis and Niall feel unloved.

Sometimes people can take quotes and make them sound worse than they are. For example, when Liam's mum told *Heat* magazine early on in the band's *X Factor* journey: 'Liam has a very strong following. I can't speak for the other boys, I don't know about their solo careers, but Liam gigged all over the country so he has both options open really,' she wasn't saying that Liam was the most talented member of the band or trying to make the others jealous: she was just talking about Liam's experience.

Niall's older brother Greg has also spoken to the press about the jealousy rumours. He told his local paper, *The Herald*: 'It's absolute nonsense. The boys all get on really well together. They instantly bonded and have become the best of friends. I'm so proud of Niall – he is getting on great. He rang a few times during the week but I don't want to talk to him because I just miss him so much. He is loving every second of the experience and the lads are all fantastic… they have a huge amount of respect for each other. They have gelled so well that it's like they have already known each other for 10 years.'

Jokes

Louis is the funniest member of One Direction and he's forever telling bad jokes. He is a comedy genius sometimes and always made the other *X Factor* contestants laugh when they were missing home. Louis loves practical jokes and managed to pull a good one on Liam during an outside photo shoot.

Liam explained what happened to the *Shropshire Star*: 'We were playing football outside and the football went into the pond. I went to get the football out of the pond and one of the boys pushed me in.

'I think it was Louis – but it meant I got free clothes because they didn't want the clothes back. I'm glad he pushed me in, I got some nice free jeans out of it.'

If Liam thinks of something that will make someone laugh, he just goes ahead and does it. The other boys like joking around, too. When Liam and Harry were tired of waiting outside their *X Factor* rehearsal studio, they decided that they needed to do something and found a huge cardboard box to play in. Harry sat inside and once Liam closed it up, photographers had to guess who was inside. The only clue was the hand popping up through a gap in the

LIAM AND HARRY MESS
AROUND DURING A BREAK
FROM REHEARSALS.

cardboard. Liam then did the big reveal and the boys couldn't stop laughing.

The band mates probably survived the long hours in the studio, day after day, because they're so good humoured and are willing to have fun. They might be serious once rehearsals began, but afterwards they would think of something amusing to do. Louis was often put in charge of the interviews and quizzes for *The X Factor* website and he would put on a fake American presenter's voice. The other contestants would be crying with laughter because he was so funny. He enjoyed making two contestants go head to head and then, when it came to revealing the winner, he would say that it was Harry – even though he wasn't taking part. You should visit the website and check them out – http://xfactor.itv.com.

The other contestants loved sharing *The X Factor* house with the boys because they were so funny all the time. Matt thinks that Zayn is the funniest member of One Direction. It really cracks him up when Zayn says 'What's happening?' with a strong accent – he says it all the time. Katie can't pick a single band mate: she thinks every member of One Direction is funny. Cher thinks it's Louis because he's always telling jokes and that makes her smile – she thinks he's the bee's knees.

In one of her *X Factor* weekly videos, Mary admitted: 'Louis, he's up for anything. Even when

Konnie [Huq] comes in to do a bit of a joke with him, he's on the ball. He works hard, but he's relaxed and funny behind the scenes. He's hilarious, the stuff he comes out with just makes you laugh, makes you feel good.'

Judges' Houses

Simon invited eight groups over to Spain to compete to be one of his three acts for *The X Factor* live shows. Liam, Harry, Zayn, Niall and Louis all practised for weeks under the watchful gaze of their parents but they had to do the Judges' Houses round on their own. As they boarded the plane, they only had each other for support.

On arrival at Simon's rented villa in Marbella, the boys were stunned: it was a truly amazing place. There were 20 bedrooms, a home cinema and three swimming pools. It would have been easy for them to get distracted but they remained focused and concentrated on practising their song, again and again.

When Louis hurt his foot and was rushed to hospital, the remaining band mates were forced to think about performing as a four-piece. Zayn admitted at the time: 'We're all panicking a little bit 'cos we're not sure what's going to happen or when he's going to get here.' Liam added: 'For us that's really bad as we haven't had that

THE BOYS WERE INVITED TO THE SIMON'S HOUSE IN MARBELLA FOR THE FINAL ROUND OF AUDITIONS.

much time to practise as we've only just got together as a group. I hope he's back as we really do need him.'

Thankfully, he arrived back just in time. The reunited five-piece performed the Natalie Imbruglia song 'Torn': Liam sang the verse and Harry did the chorus. Niall and Louis harmonised and Zayn finished the song. It was a team effort, but they played to their strengths, too. After the boys had walked off, Simon told his helper Sinitta: 'They're cool, they're relevant.' He could tell that the boys were a bit nervous but he still thought they put in a great performance.

Harry told the camera: 'Your hunger for it grows and grows as you get through each stage in the competition. It's just the biggest stage to be told "yes" or "no"… it's one word that can change your life forever because it won't be the same if you get a "yes" and if you get a "no", then it's straight back to doing stuff that kind of drives you to come here in the first place.'

Here are the groups they were up against and the songs Simon Cowell picked for them:

Twem sang Kelly Rowland's 'When Love Takes Over'

Belle Amie sang George Michael's 'Faith'

Princes & Rogues sang 'Video Killed The Radio Star'

Husstle sang 'Tainted Love'

The Reason sang Daniel Bedingfield's 'If You're Not The One'

FYD sang 'Beggin'' by Madcon

Diva Fever sang 'Love Machine' by Girls Aloud

A few of the groups disappointed Simon because he'd expected them to sing better than they did, but you could tell that One Direction had impressed him big time. It made picking his top three even harder.

When Simon had made his decision, he called all the acts in, one by one, to let them know their fate. He told Zayn, Louis, Liam, Niall and Harry: 'My head is saying it's a risk and my heart is saying that you deserve a shot. And that's why it's been difficult so I've made a decision. Guys, I've gone with my heart, you're through!'

The boys started screaming and then had a massive hug. Harry couldn't contain his excitement and quickly ran over to hug Simon, closely followed by Niall and Zayn. Niall, Harry and Louis all had tears in their eyes as it sunk in that they would be taking part in the live *X Factor* shows. Simon told them: 'I am so impressed with all of you, I mean that.'

It was the best moment of the boys' lives (so far), even better than finding out at Boot Camp that he was giving them a second chance. If only they knew then what was to come in December!

The boys might have enjoyed Marbella but Simon ended up having to foot a huge bill. The *Daily Mail* reported that some of the other hopefuls trashed his villa. The reports stated that some of his special champagne and Sapporo beer had been drunk. They were so loud that Simon was woken up and he wasn't amused, telling reporters that he might make the culprits pay for it out of their royalties if they made it.

K is for...

Konnie Huq

Konnie Huq is the presenter of the *Xtra Factor*. She replaced Holly Willoughby, who stepped down in the summer of 2010 to focus on her *This Morning* job. Konnie was thrilled to become the *Xtra Factor* host and even put her wedding and baby plans on hold so she could do the show.

Konnie got on well with all the boys but she seemed to have a soft spot for Harry. She picked him to be her first undercover mole in *The X Factor* house. His mission was to find out who was the vainest contestant without getting spotted. He went through all their rooms, found Cher's fake eyelashes, Katie's beads, spotted John in his pants and even put Rebecca from Belle Amie's pink bra

X Factor PRESENTER KONNIE HUQ.

on his head! In the end he named Zayn as the winner because of his collection of tongs, wipes, hairbrushes and afro comb.

The *Xtra Factor* presenter actually predicted early on that the boys would do really well in the competition and on 2 November 2010, she told the audience at the Cosmopolitan Ultimate Women of the Year awards: 'Everywhere I go, girls come up to me – even when they're not young girls but grown women – and say, "Oh my gosh, One Direction are amazing!"

'When I'm out and about, everyone is "One

Direction this, One Direction that. I like Harry, I like Zayn, I like Louis." There are five of them so if you think about it, there's one for everyone.'

It was early on when Konnie said this and there were still a lot of acts left in the competition. She also said that Simon was confident that the boys would win, but Cheryl might get the hat trick because her girls were strong, too.

During one of Konnie's *Xtra Factor* shows, Simon Cowell made a big blunder in forgetting Zayn's name. During the viewers' question section, he had just called Cheryl childish for blowing a raspberry when Dannii had an idea. She leaned over the table and asked Simon, 'What are the names of One Direction? That's our next question, Simon.'

Cheryl loved it and seemed to know that he wouldn't be able to answer. He paused and then said: 'Niall, Louis, Harry, Liam and Olly.' The audience booed, at which point Konnie quickly stepped in and told him the answer. He continued: 'Zayn, Zayn, Harry, Liam… you're confusing me now.' Konnie hinted that he only said Olly to wind the others up and most One Direction fans believe him because he's been very hands-on with the boys. He saw them several times a week during *The X Factor* live shows, helped them choose their song each week, watched them rehearse and oversaw the weekly technical rehearsal, too.

L is for...

Liam Payne

Born on 29 August 1993, Liam is one of the oldest members of One Direction and he comes from Wolverhampton. Before entering *The X Factor* he was a student at St Peter's Collegiate. He always wanted to be a performer, as he explained to the backstage *X Factor* camera: 'I've always loved singing, it's something I've always done, ever since I first got up on karaoke when I was at holiday camp [he was only five at the time] and mumbled the words to Robbie Williams' "Let Me Entertain You."' His mum was so proud that she made sure someone filmed it. Liam didn't show star quality in this first performance but it wasn't long

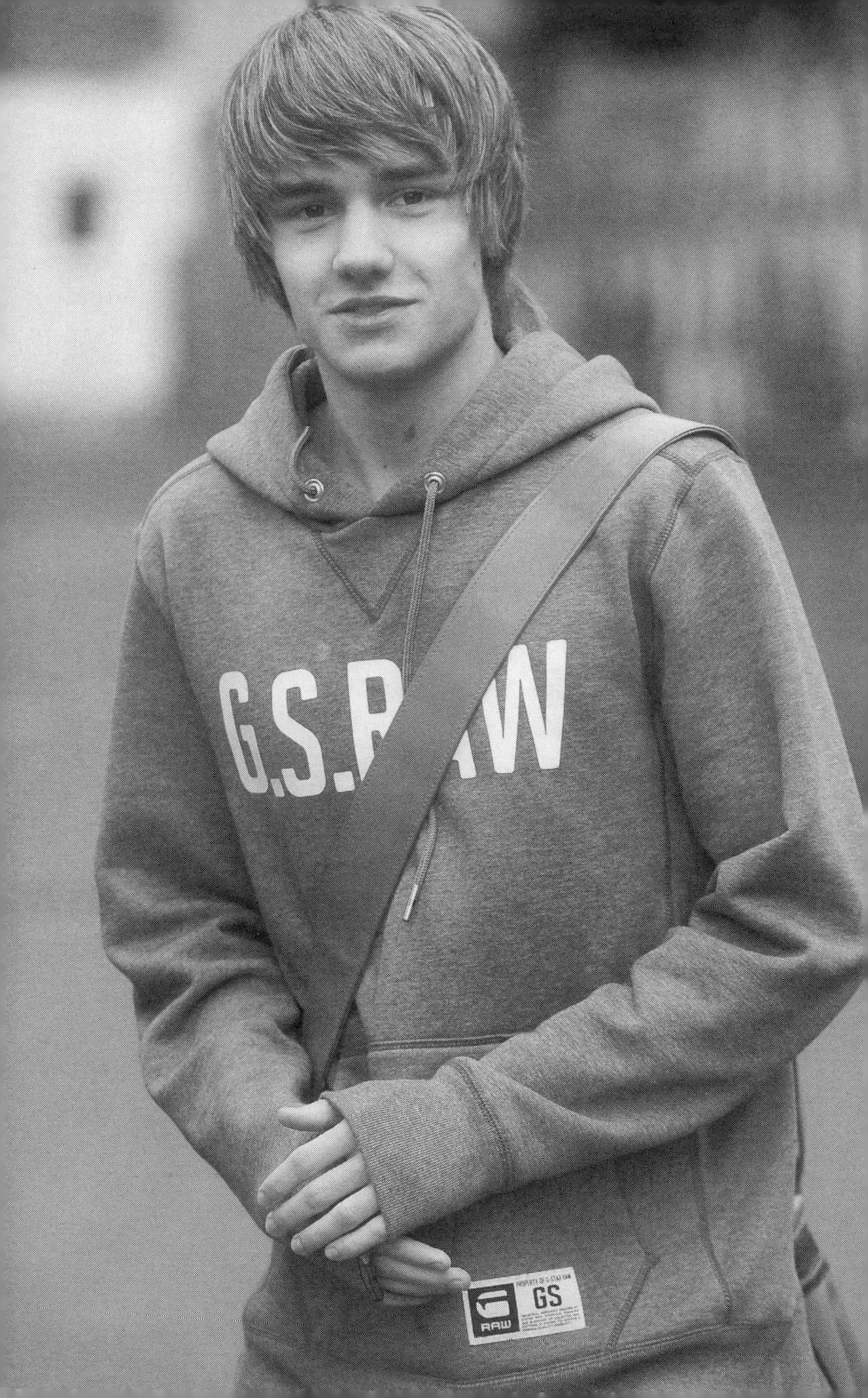
RAW
GS

before he was wowing audiences: he started to love going to karaoke nights and impressing the crowd with his powerful voice.

At the age of twelve, Liam joined Pink Productions, a performing arts group. His older sisters, Ruth and Nicola, went there, too. Liam's teacher Jodie Richards told the *Birmingham Mail*: 'Who'd have thought the Liam we see today would have nearly had to be forced onto the stage! It was clear very early that Liam was a natural talent. He gained more and more confidence with each show and took on some big singing numbers. Liam is such a lovely lad and I'm very proud to say I know him and have so many fantastic memories of him from rehearsals and personal experiences.'

It's really good that Liam continued with Pink Productions because many lads would have felt embarrassed at being in a dance/performance group made up of mostly girls during their teenage years.

Like Harry, Liam also does well at sport and was such a good runner that he represented the UK. When he was fourteen, he failed to gain a place in the England Schools team and so he decided to pursue his singing ambitions instead. He explained what happened to journalist Victoria Nash: 'I was a member of the Wolverhampton and Bilston Athletics Club and I used to get up and run five miles before school and another few miles when I came home. At that time it was always a choice between running or singing, but I just missed out on a place in the England team; I didn't enjoy the running as much as my singing and that really made my mind up for me.'

Liam auditioned for *The X Factor* in 2008 and made it to the Judges' House round. He actually went to Barbados to sing for Simon Cowell, but he didn't get through. Simon told him: 'You look almost like the perfect pop star. I've made a decision, it's bad news.' Liam was devastated: he very nearly made it but Simon decided to give someone else the opportunity. However, he told Liam to come back in a couple of years – and he did.

And so Liam went back to school but carried on singing at big events. He performed at Party in the Park in Stourbridge with another *X Factor* star Ricky Loney, appeared with Same Difference at the Wolverhampton Football Stadium, sang during a Wolves versus Man U match and supported Peter Andre, too. Every penny that he received he used to pay for his travel to London, where he had vocal lessons. He set up his own official website (www.liam-payne.com) so fans could get to know more about him and they could buy Liam sweatbands and signed photos in the merchandise section.

Liam is glad that Simon told him 'no' the first time he tried out for *The X Factor* because he wouldn't have been in One Direction otherwise and the decision also allowed him to get his GCSEs. He was studying sound technology at college but gave it up to do *The X Factor* live shows. In fact, he had been thinking about an apprenticeship at the factory where his dad works, building aeroplanes – we're so glad he didn't give up his singing dreams.

Liam had wanted to audition in 2009, but was unable to do so because the *X Factor* bosses changed the minimum age from fourteen to sixteen, so he just missed out. In the end, 2010 proved to be his year, but he still had to queue for 13 hours before his audition!

During *The X Factor* live shows, Liam only got a few days off but he made sure he used the time to travel home to see family and friends. It was fun just being Liam again, with no rehearsing, no paparazzi, just shopping and a meal at Frankie & Benny's with his family. He talked to his local paper, the *Express & Star*, about one such trip: 'It was my sister Ruth's 20th birthday so I came back to Wolverhampton and spent some time with my family. Not many people noticed me. No one knew I was going to be there. We went out for a meal at Frankie & Benny's at Merry Hill. More people noticed me there and lots of people came over for autographs and photographs.'

Liam got recognised as he walked down the street and people working in the shops even came outside and asked him to pose for photos and sign autographs. Staff at The Body Shop in particular were thrilled and told the paper: 'He seemed quite grateful for the attention – the fame has not gone to his head yet. The girls were absolutely made up.' The next day, Liam quickly made his way back to London for more rehearsals with Niall, Harry, Zayn and Louis. His mum and dad came with him, which meant they could catch up more on the journey down – they miss Liam so much when he's away from home but they're so glad he's living his dream.

FIVE FASCINATING FACTS ABOUT LIAM

He loves America and has been there 10 times

He used to spend Christmas there

Liam can play piano and guitar

He would have liked to become a PE teacher if
  he hadn't been in One Direction

Purple is his favourite colour

He likes basketball, golf and footy

Louis Tomlinson

Louis is from Bassacar in Doncaster and he's the oldest bandmate in One Direction. He was born on 24 December 1991, Christmas Eve! Unlike Liam, who

LIAM IS ONE
OF THE MOST
POPULAR MEMBERS
OF THE BAND.

started singing when he was five, Louis only really started to sing properly when he was fourteen and began singing in a band with his mates. It was then that he realised that he could sing and it made him a lot more confident. He entered local talent shows for fun and to show people his skill.

Louis also played the part of Danny Zucco in his school's production of *Grease* – you should check out his YouTube channel to see him in action: http://www.youtube.com/user/louistomlinson07. He shows off his acting and singing skills in the clips he has posted up. More recently, he wrote a message to his One Direction fans on YouTube saying: 'hiyaa eveyy 1 its louis i am so pleaseed withall yor comments... just like to say a big thankyou to hannah walker my beatifull girlfriend who has been suporting me all they wayy thanks babe xxxxxxx'

Louis has four younger sisters: twins Phoebe and Daisy, aged six, Felicite (ten) and Lottie (twelve). Phoebe and Daisy saw the boys perform for the first time in Rock Week. Until then, they had been banned from the audience because *The X Factor* has strict rules about how old you have to be to sit there. Thankfully, the rules were relaxed for Phoebe and Daisy because it would have been a shame for them to miss out on seeing their brother just because they were a year or two too young. Besides, they had been

watching the other shows with their grandparents, great grandmother and auntie at home (their living room wall was covered in a huge 'Louis has The X Factor' display and a picture of One Direction). Normally the family is given just four tickets to the show each week and so Louis' mum, dad, best friend Stan and girlfriend Hannah would go.

All the boys like Stan and enjoy seeing him each weekend. They did a shout out to Stan and Hannah's sister, Emily, in one of their weekly video diaries but just pretended they were random people.

Louis' mum Johannah is so proud of him but she finds it tough being apart. She explained to her local paper: 'We've got a close relationship. He's got four sisters and he is my only boy. He is a lovely family lad. I'm missing him loads while he's in London.' She found watching the boys' first performance very moving and revealed to the *Star*: 'It was brilliant – I could hardly remember the performance. We watched a recording of it again when we got home and that was easier to take in because we were not nervous then because it wasn't live.

'It was the biggest stage he'd ever performed on – before that the biggest show he had done was *Grease* at Hall Cross School early this year when he played Danny. That was to about 200 people – Saturday was to 14.8 million.'

Watching the final was even more emotional for Johannah and the rest of the boys' mums. Naturally, they wanted their sons to win so much and felt sick with nerves as they didn't want their dreams to be dashed.

Louis had just finished his AS-levels when he auditioned for the *X Factor* – it was a bit of a step up from the talent shows, but he thought it was worth a try. He never returned to college in the September because he was too busy rehearsing for the live shows with Liam, Harry, Niall and Zayn. If he ever wants to go back and do his A2 Theatre Studies, English Literature and PE exams so that he's got his AS-Levels to fall back on, he could still do so but no one at his college is holding their breath. He's a huge star now and it looks like he's going to be so busy writing and recording songs for One Direction's first album.

On 5 November 2010, the *Sun* reported that the boys had been given two hours off, but Louis had travelled all the way home to Doncaster and didn't return until the next day. One Direction fans didn't blame him – he just needed to see his family. Meanwhile, the *Sun* said *X Factor* bosses were furious.

Louis misses his girlfriend Hannah loads now he's living in London but she visited the *X Factor* set every weekend and they got to spend a small amount of time together. Now that the series is over, they should be

LOUIS ARRIVES AT A FILM
PREMIERE BY LIMOUSINE.

able to see more of each other because Louis' schedule won't be so tightly packed.

FIVE FASCINATING FACTS ABOUT LOUIS:

He owns a 'Superman' T-shirt and has worn it after Sunday night results and pretended to be Clark Kent in one video diary – he's *our* Superman!

Performing with Robbie Williams in the final was a dream come true

He can play the piano

If he wasn't in One Direction, he would have liked to work on a farm

In the past, he's been a football coach, worked at a cinema and on the tills at Doncaster Football Stadium

M is for...

Mary Byrne

Warm-hearted Mary Byrne from Ireland really looked after the boys when they were living in the *X Factor* house and they were gutted to see her go home in the semi-final. She really took to the boys the second she met them and became their surrogate mother during *X Factor* journeys.

She told the *Daily Mirror*: 'From the day we moved in, I've always got a kiss off each of the boys every morning. I'm just a child at heart and I can come down to their level and relate to the things they do – they lift your spirits so much.

'We do have some craic together. I have the same wacky sense of humour.'

ZAYN AND LOUIS SHOW THEIR LOVE FOR MARY BYRNE, ONE DIRECTION'S FAVOURITE IRISH SINGER.

Mary felt as if she had five teenage sons while living in the *X Factor* house. She kept asking the boys to tidy their room because it was so messy, but they rarely did. Instead, she found herself cleaning up after them and folding their clean clothes. It made her realise that her daughter wasn't so messy at all, compared to them. She

171

will be keeping in touch with the band and wishes them all the best.

Miming

During *The X Factor* some people suggested that the boys mimed during their performances, but this wasn't the case at all: the bandmates wouldn't have been putting in 18-hour days if that were the case. For the performances on a Sunday night alongside the other contestants, they had to mime alongside everyone else because the group performances were of secondary importance. Everyone spent the week rehearsing their own song so there was little time to rehearse the group number; they were also energetic performances and to sing live might have made them sound bad. The public isn't asked to vote after the group performance so it didn't really matter – but for their individual songs it did.

One Direction were first accused of miming after their 'Kids in America' performance. The camera had focused on Zayn and it looked as if he'd missed his cue but you could still hear the words. But he wasn't miming, it was Harry's voice: he was singing, too but the camera had zoomed in on Zayn so you couldn't see Harry. Poor Zayn faced a lot of criticism on Twitter later that night.

RoseGardenAcs tweeted: 'One Direction miming the chorus. I'd send them straight to the naughty step.'

Alexander McNeil also thought they were miming: 'Zayn REALLY dropped the ball on The #xfactor tonight.... so obviously One Direction were miming parts... ARGH!'

It must have been upsetting for the boys because they'd given an amazing performance and deserved to be praised, not accused of cheating. All *The X Factor* singers are thought to have used pre-recorded vocals as backing tracks each week but it's nothing unusual in the music business.

A few weeks later an article in the *Sun* suggested that former *X Factor* winner Shayne Ward believed that the boys were miming. It alleged that he said: 'They shouldn't mime, but there has to be a reason. With *X Factor* you do loads of interviews – a lot of talking so when it comes to the weekend, voices are shot. You can tell they're hurting because they don't want to mime. Not that I ever did it.'

Shayne was upset when he saw the story and set the record straight on Twitter. He tweeted: 'One Direction are great and have my backing. I never said they were miming, I don't need to defend myself. If you must know, a journalist said they were and asked my take on miming. That's the real story end of.'

FORMER *X FACTOR* CONTESTANT SHAYNE WARD GAVE HIS BACKING TO ONE DIRECTION AFTER HIS APPEARANCE ON THE SHOW.

Music

Liam, Harry, Louis, Zayn and Niall are all passionate about music: they love to sing and they love to listen to it. They couldn't imagine their lives without music and being on *The X Factor* has made them listen to music that they wouldn't have necessarily listened to before. 2010 was an absolutely incredible year for the boys and there are three tracks that stood out for them. The first one is 'Billionaire' by Travie McCoy, the second one is 'Firework' by Katy Perry and their third favourite was 'Please Don't Let Me Go' by Olly Murs. They loved the tracks before they even got to meet Katy Perry and Olly Murs – they think they're the best of 2010.

During their time on the show they were asked which songs they listen to when they want to be motivated. They picked the classic 'Eye Of The Tiger' by Survivor, Eminem's 'Not Afraid' and 'Harder, Better, Faster, Stronger' by Daft Punk. Sometimes it's quite difficult for them to pick a top three because there are five of them in the band and they have very different musical tastes. When they lived in *The X Factor* house they could listen to almost any track they wanted because there was a massive jukebox with hundreds of songs saved on its memory. If they wanted to calm down after a long day and just chill, they would pick 'Breakeven' by The Script, Robbie Williams' 'She's The One' or 'Fix You' by Coldplay.

Being a lot younger than the average boy band means the boys can't go clubbing or drinking – not that they would have had time for that while they were doing *The X Factor* live shows anyway. If they were having a house party or going to a friend's birthday party, they told Ovi Music Store that there are three songs they would request to get people on the dancefloor. Liam, Harry, Louis, Niall and Zayn love 'I Bet You Look Good On the Dancefloor' by Arctic Monkeys, Nelly's 'Hot In Here' and 'Thriller' by Michael Jackson. All three tracks are good fun to dance to.

The boys were asked to pick their top three eighties tracks and even though none of them were born during that decade, they still managed to come up with some cracking songs. They picked 'Bad' by Michael Jackson, 'Jessie's Girl' by George Michael and once again, Michael Jackson's 'Thriller'.

From their very first auditions to Boot Camp, to Judges' Houses to live shows, the songs that the boys sang during their time on *The X Factor* will always be special and remind them of good times. They won't be able to sing all their favourite tunes during The X Factor Live Tour, which kicks off in Birmingham on 20 February 2011 but once they've released their first album, they will be looking to doing an arena tour of their own. Then they'll be able to sing all their favourites, plus tracks they have written themselves – One Direction fans can't wait!

N is for...

Naked

Our favourite boys aren't afraid to show off their bodies – they are forever stripping off. Even before Harry joined the band, he would walk round in his boxers all the time (hopefully he covered up when his sister Gemma had mates around!).

In November 2010, the boys had good fun filming 'Harry's naked problem' for the *Xtra Factor*. In the video the boys sit around the kitchen table talking to the camera while Harry (naked) makes himself some cereal. Louis tells the camera: 'I'm really, really worried about Harry, I feel like he's going nuts. He just can't, he just can't keep his clothes on and it's interrupting our practices. How are we supposed to concentrate when he's walking around in the nude?' Liam adds: 'We just want to be singers, good singers, and we're trying to concentrate and he's getting naked every time. There's absolutely nothing we can do about it.' Louis: 'He's always in the nude!'

While Liam and Louis were talking, a naked Harry moved around the kitchen, his privates hidden by various things. The clever bit was when he moved to the table and Zayn was looking through an *X Factor* book: he passed it to Niall and as he did so, Harry moved at the same time so his privates were still hidden. To end the video, Harry grabbed the book off Niall and moved out of the camera's range. It must have taken them a few takes to get it right!

In another episode, Harry was also filmed sitting up on the top bunk of his bed, stark naked. The only thing covering his modesty was an *Xtra Factor* logo (added on, post production). Although the clip only lasted a couple of seconds, the fans loved it. One called it 'the best two seconds of my life!'

Harry isn't the only one in the band to get naked on a regular basis, though. The boys told the *Daily Star:* 'We have trouble keeping our clothes on. We've always got our kit off in *The X Factor* house we love a bit of skin flashing. Even now we fancy a strip and we reckon Louis Walsh wants us to, too!' It's a good job all the boys are comfortable with their bodies because sharing one small room in *The X Factor* house meant that they didn't have much privacy at all.

Niall Horan

Niall is one of the cheekiest members of One Direction and he's always smiling. Born on 13 September 1993, he is from Mullingar in Ireland. Niall started singing when he was really young and by the time he was eight, his teacher had spotted that he was a talented singer and told him to take singing seriously. Two years later, he got the performing bug. As he explained to *The X Factor* cameras: 'I've always sung and when I was about ten, I played Oliver in the school play and I just always remember being really happy on stage.' After that, Niall decided to enter talent shows at his school and every year he would put his name forward. He also started to sing and act at the Mullingar Arts Centre.

In November 2009, Niall entered a local talent competition – Mullingar Shamrocks' show, 'Stars In Their Eyes' – where he impersonated Jason Mraz and sang his track, 'I'm Yours'. The crowd went wild. As Niall sang and played guitar, they started screaming and singing along. It was an amazing performance and everyone knew then that he had the potential to be a

big star. At the end, lots of people rushed over to ask for his autograph.

Niall decided to enter *The X Factor* on 13 December 2009 – the night Joe McElderry won. After the show, he went straight online and registered for an audition. Seeing Joe win inspired him to give it a go and also winning the 'Stars In Their Eyes' competition made him realise how much he wanted to be a professional singer. A few weeks later, he was invited to be a warm up act for *X Factor* star Lloyd Daniels (who finished in fifth place in *The X Factor* 2009). As he belted out Justin Timberlake's 'Cry Me A River' in front of thousands of people, Niall didn't seem nervous at all.

While queuing up for his audition, Niall kept the crowds entertained by singing Justin Bieber's 'One Time'. He had brought his guitar along, so he played as he sang. The girls standing next to him were so impressed that they filmed him playing (they must have known then that he would go far in the competition). You can see the video they took on YouTube, if you type in 'Niall Horan One Time'. When Niall entered the show, he was looking forward to getting attention from gorgeous girls, making an album, going on tour and singing on live TV every week!

Before Niall appeared on *The X Factor* he was just a normal schoolboy living at home. His family and close friends hated having to keep how well he was doing a secret until *The X Factor* shows were broadcast on TV: they didn't keep his big brother up to date at all because they were scared he'd tell people that Niall had made it to the live shows before the Judges' Houses episodes were shown on TV. If his brother had told people, Niall might have been kicked out of One Direction.

Niall's proud dad Bobby told his local paper: 'He is very witty and good-humoured. He could probably do a better Geordie accent than Cheryl Cole!'

Mum Maura had never thought of Niall as anything but a solo artist but she is so glad that he's in One Direction. She is separated from Niall's father and lives in Edgeworthstown, which isn't too far away from Mullingar. During an interview with the *Westmeath Examiner*, Maura said: 'He's a light-hearted lad. One thing I do know is that he is completely committed and focused on his singing. He'd sing for his breakfast, dinner and tea!'

Niall's local fans were looking forward to seeing One Direction switch on the Christmas lights, but the boys had to cancel at the last minute because they were too busy rehearsing their two songs for Rock Week. Niall and the others hated letting people down but they couldn't afford to miss out on vital rehearsal time. His dad was gutted they couldn't fly over: he works in the local Tesco store and all his customers and colleagues were looking forward to seeing Niall perform. Every week, they asked how he was getting on and they had been voting for One Direction.

Bobby told the *Herald*: 'Everyone is very interested in them, there has been great support.'

Sometimes Niall feels like he's dreaming. His dad sums it up when he says: 'It's surreal when you see it, we're just ordinary people. It's like doing the Lotto, you don't expect to win it and he didn't expect to go so far, but they're still there.' Niall has never had a job and so it will be even more amazing for him when he gets his first royalty cheque.

FIVE FASCINATING FACTS ABOUT NIALL

If Niall was made of chocolate, he'd be a Terry's Chocolate Orange

He can play guitar and likes bringing his own to *The X Factor* studios on a Saturday morning

His middle name is Timothy

When he was little, he had an army outfit with a helmet that he liked to wear and he had a huge gun that was almost as big as he was!

His town had huge 'Niall Horan One Direction' signs put on their recycling bin wagons during *The X Factor* to encourage people to vote for him

Number 1s – Week One

The first live show was extremely nerve wracking for all twelve acts picked at Judges' Houses and at the start of the show, the four wildcards who were revealed. The boys had been rehearsing for weeks, but Zayn was having problems coming in on time and worried that it could happen in the live show and he might ruin things for Harry, Niall, Liam and Louis. He didn't want to make them go home in Week One! Thankfully, Zayn made it on time and the boys gave a solid performance of 'Viva La Vida'.

WHO SANG WHAT

Matt Cardle – 'When Love Takes Over' by David Guetta

Nicolo Festa – 'Just Dance' by Lady Gaga

Aiden Grimshaw – 'Mad World' by Tears For Fears

Paije Richardson – 'Killing Me Softly' by the Fugees

Rebecca Ferguson – 'Teardrop' by Womack & Womack

Treyc Cohen – 'One' by U2

Cher Lloyd – 'Just Be Good To Me' by Beats International

Katie Waissel – 'We Are The Champions' by Queen

Mary Byrne – 'It's A Man's Man's Man's World' by James Brown

Storm – 'We Built This City On Rock and Roll' by Starship

John Adeleye – 'One Sweet Day' by Mariah Carey and Boyz II Men

Wagner – 'She Bangs' by Ricky Martin and 'Love Shack' by the B-52s medley

FYD – 'Billionaire' by Travie McCoy feat. Bruno Mars

Diva Fever – 'Sunny' by Bobby Hebb

Belle Amie – 'Airplanes' by B.O.B

One Direction – Viva La Vida by Coldplay

WHAT THE JUDGES THOUGHT

Louis Walsh: 'Wow guys, when I heard you were going to do Coldplay I thought it was a big, big risk! I love what you did with the song – you totally made it your own. I love that the band is gelling, even though Simon's going to claim he put this band together: it was my idea originally, Simon. It *was*! Boys, I think potentially you could be the next big boy band, but you have a lot of work to do. But Simon Cowell, I'm not sure about the styling! Did you have a stylist?'

Dannii Minogue: 'Guys, I don't know whose idea it

was because I wasn't there, but you look like you fit together, like you're the perfect band. That song was fantastic and you did make it your own. I wasn't thinking of Coldplay then, it was the perfect pop band performance.'

Cheryl Cole: 'I have to agree with Dannii, you look like you were meant to be together as a group. You look fantastic – you've got all the ingredients of the perfect pop band. I reckon the girls will be going crazy for you, but you need a little bit more time to develop as a group, that's all. Just a little bit more time.'

Simon: 'Regarding your role in putting the group together, Louis, we'll rewind the tapes on that one. You guys came together because your Boot Camp auditions weren't good enough but you were too good to throw away. We took a risk, and I've got to tell you, what was so impressive about that was when you started to screw up: one of you at the end, Liam stepped in, you brought it back together. That's what bands do. Regarding the whole styling issue, Louis: I don't want to style this band because I don't know how to style a band like this. We asked the band to do whatever they wanted to do – I'm not going to interfere, they're going to do it their way. It was brilliant, guys!'

WHAT THE BOYS THOUGHT

Zayn told the backstage camera: 'We came off the stage after our performance, we were all buzzing. I don't know how to describe what it was like because you will never understand what it was like until you've actually performed on the stage. It was just amazing!'

And they were so glad that they weren't in the sing-off and looked forward to the challenges of Week Two.

THE SING-OFF

Nicolo Festa received the lowest votes so he left automatically and became the first act to leave the show. The sing-off was between Katie and FYD. Katie sang 'Don't Let Me Down' by The Beatles and FYD chose Rihanna's 'Please Don't Stop The Music'. Simon voted to save his own act – FYD – but the other judges all voted for Katie. FYD therefore became the second act to leave the show.

FYD WERE THE SECOND ACT TO LEAVE *THE X FACTOR.*

O is for...

One Direction

When Simon, Louis and Nicole Scherzinger put the boys together at Boot Camp they didn't give them a name. They wanted Liam, Louis, Harry, Zayn and Niall to come up with their own name to reflect who they were. This presented the boys with a problem because it's really hard to think of a unique name for a band that sounds good. All too often bands come up with a name only to be told there's another band with the same name and so they have to change it.

All the boys had a think and came up with names, but it was Harry who thought up One Direction. It just popped into Harry's head! The others all agreed that it was a great name and that was that. Simon thought the name was good too, otherwise he would have told them to have another think. One Direction sums them up: they all wanted the same thing and they were all going in one direction – straight to the top of the charts!

For the boys, being on stage and performing is the best thing about being in the band. Liam told *The X Factor* cameras during the live shows: 'Being on stage is absolutely amazing! I mean, we only spend such a short time on it but we love absolutely every second of it. We wouldn't change any of it, it's great!'

And the boys feel so lucky that Simon handpicked each of them to be in the band. He could have just chosen four bandmates as he did for Belle Amie but he had a good feeling about all five of them. Zayn admitted to *The X Factor* website: 'This for us is just unbelievable! We were all sat in the car today and I think it was Liam that said, "It feels like a dream and that we're all going to wake up and our mums are gonna be like, 'Wake up, get ready for school' kind of thing."'

Louis continued: 'I think it's easy for people at home to look at us and think we're just having fun. The reason we're having fun is because we're working hard.'

All the boys have different personalities but everyone gets on. It's great that each of them brings something new to the group. Louis thinks that Liam is the smart one, Harry is the flirty one, Zayn is the vain one and

Niall is the funny one. He couldn't think of a word to describe his own character so Harry picked 'leader'. Liam summed up the dynamics of the group in an interview with the *Shropshire Star*: 'The dynamic of our band is that there are loud people and there are quiet people, and there are people in between – I would say I am probably one of the in-between people and one of the quiet people. But we all get on so well, it's unbelievable. Everyone is just so happy to be here, we just have a laugh 24/7. It is hard to get to sleep at night – everyone just carries on joking about.'

There are times when they argue, though. Louis told Digital Spy: 'Because we're around each other so often it's like arguing with your siblings. You fall out with them, go away and have a bit of a paddy, then come back and get over it.'

Liam added: 'I think every band has arguments but the funny thing is, you just get over them really quickly – they last about five minutes. You just get over it because you know we're all going for the same thing so you just put your differences aside and get on with it.'

If someone does cause an argument then they quickly apologise so the band can move on. Zayn confessed: 'I like making up by going to McDonald's and buying a takeaway for the lads just to show I'm their mate. I've done it a couple of times!'

Virtually from day one, One Direction decided that

they would stay together, even if they were voted off early on in the competition. With each live show, they realised even more how much they wanted to be a band and vowed to keep on going. Not many bands manage to do that once they leave *The X Factor*. The boys didn't want to go back to college to study for their A-levels: they wanted to be the next big boy band. Even if they didn't win, they were eager to be like JLS and get a record deal. In November 2010, reports suggested they were guaranteed a record deal whether they won the show or not, and that musical producers had already started writing songs for them. But this wasn't true and Liam took to Twitter just to set the record straight. He tweeted: 'The rumours about us getting offered a deal aren't true, we need your help to win this, so please keep voting guys x.'

P is for...

Paparazzi

When the boys started their *X Factor* journeys they hadn't even thought about the paparazzi following them. They knew that the paparazzi followed celebrities but it took a while for it to sink in that they themselves were now famous. Just going to the corner shop became a big event with paparazzi following them inside and taking photos of what they were buying. Soon, they couldn't hide anywhere in London because the paparazzi followed them all day. Once they left *The X Factor* house in the morning, the paparazzi would be waiting at the bottom of the road and when they came back late at night, they would be there, too.

Liam told the *Shropshire Star*: 'It's weird when we go out sometimes and we get chased by paparazzi out the car. There will be about eight photographers there, just taking photos of you walking down the street. It's very, very weird. It's hard to get used to, but it's cool.'

Sometimes the paparazzi are tipped off so they find out where Liam, Louis, Zayn, Niall and Harry are going to be. On 20 October 2010, all the remaining *X Factor* contestants were invited to Topman/Topshop in London's West End to go on a massive shopping spree – for free! They could choose whatever they wanted and they all walked out with bags full of clothes. It was quite overwhelming for the boys when they arrived because the street outside was packed with screaming fans and they struggled to even get in the store. Once inside, the place was even more cramped as the sheer volume of fans and photographers made it hard to move around and actually look at the clothes on the racks. They smiled for photos and signed as many autographs as possible but it was impossible to do this for everyone because there were so many people there. As they were escorted to their car, they reflected on a busy night and once again felt like they were in a dream.

The boys are going to have to get used to being followed by the paparazzi because they will be pursuing them for as long as they are One Direction – the hottest boy band in the world!

Premieres

Every celebrity goes to premieres, whether they are connected to the film industry or not. The boys were over the moon when they were invited to the *Harry Potter and the Deathly Hallows* premiere in Leicester Square on 11 November. It was the biggest premiere of 2010. They all got ready at the exclusive Dorchester Hotel and waited in a room while the cars to transport them to the red carpet were being arranged.

The bandmates were just chatting among themselves when Daniel Radcliffe came in and introduced himself. Louis and Harry were speechless for a change! They might have expected to catch a glimpse of him on the red carpet, but they never imagined they'd get to have a conversation with him. Although they quickly thought of some questions to ask, the whole situation was very surreal. Louis asked Daniel how fit Hermione is. In return, Daniel said 'very' but that she was like a sister to him. It's a good job that Louis said 'Hermione' in his question not Emma Watson as his girlfriend might have been upset!

Later on, when they actually arrived at the premiere they bumped into Emma and had a brief chat. The boys admitted on camera that they'd had crushes on her when they were younger – they all seemed to love the *Harry Potter* movies and books. Later, Emma told the backstage camera that she was supporting One Direction.

The next day was a Friday, which meant dress rehearsals for everyone. Zayn, Liam, Louis, Harry and Niall were so tired because they hadn't got in till late and they had to get up at 6am. They just wanted to go back to bed, but they had to get to The Fountain Studios as soon as possible. It was their last full day of rehearsals before they had to perform 'Something About The Way You Look Tonight' on the live show and they wanted it to be perfect.

The second premiere that the boys attended was during the semi-final week. This time, they enjoyed mixing with the celebrities at *The Chronicles Of Narnia: The Voyage of the Dawn Treader*. It was snowing and HM the Queen was there – it really was a special night. It was nice for them to spend time outside of a rehearsal room because they'd been cooped up in there all week. They got to speak to *The X Factor* 2009 winner Joe McElderry and he even offered them some advice. Just knowing that he recorded one of the songs in the movie made the boys realise what opportunities might come their way in the future.

THE BOYS
ARRIVE FOR A
FILM PREMIERE
IN LONDON.

Q is for...

Questions

Sometimes journalists and TV presenters can ask the boys really boring questions but fans never do. Indeed, the boys were asked some great questions by fans in their weekly *X Factor* diary video. One fan asked them what superpower they would pick. Louis said he'd like to fly, Liam wanted to be invisible, Zayn wants to stay young forever – 'Eternal youth, it would be sick' – and Harry would like to time travel.

In the same video, they were asked about their strangest dreams. Harry admitted when he was six, he had dreamt that rats bit all his toes off. Yuck! When Zayn was eight years old, he had a dream that a giant

Power Ranger was chasing him (Zayn, Niall and Louis all loved Power Rangers when they were growing up). Louis' strangest dream was one that he kept having over and over: in his dream, he would go to school but when he looked down he would realise that he didn't have any clothes on!

In their *X Factor* Week Four video diary, Liam was asked what he would bathe in, if he couldn't pick water – he said, 'icing sugar'. That was probably the most random thing they've ever been asked!

Another great question from a fan that the boys have answered in the past was which celebrity they would like to swap places with for the day. Liam would like to be Michael McIntyre because he's a comedy genius, Niall would pick singer Michael Bublé because he's such a legend and Zayn would like to be the King of Cool, David Beckham. Louis would pick Susan Boyle, while Harry prefers David Hasselhoff.

During one of their video diaries, the boys answered a question set by Shannon, one of their fans. She wanted to know if they could be a single member of the band for one day, who would they pick? Louis said he'd be Harry because he'd like to have curly hair, Liam likes the way Niall views life so he'd choose him, Zayn and Niall want to be Louis because they think he's hilarious. Meanwhile, Harry opted for Zayn because he thinks he's clever and funny.

R is for...

'Rock' – Week Seven

In Week Seven, the final seven acts had to sing two rock-themed songs. It was a very stressful week for all the acts involved because they had to rehearse two songs for the Saturday show, plus they needed a third song in case they were in the sing-off and they knew that two acts would be going home on the Sunday. This had not been the original plan and all the acts involved only found out at the last minute. The act that received the lowest number of votes would go automatically and then the second and third from bottom would have to sing again. Of course, no one wanted to be in the bottom three.

WHO SANG WHAT

Matt Cardle – 'I Love Rock'n'Roll' by Joan Jett and the Blackhearts and 'Nights In White Satin' by The Moody Blues

Rebecca Ferguson – 'I Still Haven't Found What I'm Looking For' by U2 and 'I Can't Get No Satisfaction' by Aretha Franklin

Katie Waissel – 'Everybody Hurts' by REM and 'Sex On Fire' by Kings of Leon

Cher Lloyd – 'Walk This Way' by Run DMC/Aerosmith and 'Girlfriend' by Avril Lavigne

Wagner – 'Creep' by Radiohead and 'Addicted To Love' by Robert Palmer

Mary Byrne – 'All I Want Is You' by U2 and 'Brass In Pocket' by The Pretenders

One Direction – 'Summer Of '69' by Bryan Adams and 'You Are So Beautiful' by Joe Cocker

WHAT THE JUDGES THOUGHT:

Performance One – 'Summer Of '69'

Louis Walsh: 'Hey boys, that absolutely worked! I love the choice of song, I love the vibe, the vitality you bring to the competition. The competition would not be the same without One Direction. I love the way that you've gelled as friends. I think you're the next big boy band.'

ONE DIRECTION SANG 'SUMMER OF '69' BY BRYAN ADAMS DURING THE ROCK WEEK EDITION OF *THE X FACTOR*.

Dannii Minogue: 'You've clearly done lots of work and really stepped it up, I like that.'

Cheryl Cole: 'We've got feet stamps going on, there's electricity in the room, it's fantastic... You just keep growing and growing, and getting better and better. I think there's a big future for you, congratulations.'

Simon Cowell: 'I had nothing to do with this song choice – Harry chose the song, great choice of song. Just remember next week is the semi-final: you've worked your butts off to get where you've got to – you've got to be there next week! Please pick up the phone.'

DID YOU KNOW?

Harry picked the song because it was the first song that he ever performed with his band, White Eskimo. He was so glad that Simon and the boys thought it was a good choice.

Performance Two – 'You Are So Beautiful'
Louis Walsh: 'Wow boys, you've proven tonight you're not just another boy band, you're a brilliant, brilliant vocal group and you've proved that everybody in this group can sing, which is incredible! I love the song – I love everything about it. I don't think it's a rock song, Simon – it's in the rules – but it *is* a brilliant song. It's not really a rock song, is it?'

Dannii Minogue: 'Guys, there's one word for that and that's stunning. Absolutely wonderful.'

Cheryl Cole: 'It's great to see you having fun, and having all the dancers and all of that. I love that side of you, but I absolutely loved you standing and hearing

you sing. It's what it's all about. You should be able to do everything and I think you've got a really bright future as a boy band, I really do.'

Simon Cowell: 'This was in some ways my favourite performance by you because it was beautifully sung and Zayn, in particular. I can remember back at Boot Camp and I had to get you from the back because you were too embarrassed to dance and I've seen how you've transformed, found your confidence and how the boys have looked after you. Genuinely, I am so proud of you tonight, congratulations.'

WHAT THE BOYS THOUGHT:

The boys have never been big headed and they genuinely believed they might be in the sing-off. By the time Dermot O'Leary called One Direction, there were only four acts on the stage and they were the last act to be guaranteed a place in

WAGNER BECAME THE ELEVENTH ACT TO LEAVE THE SHOW DURING ROCK WEEK.

the semi-final. Louis confided in the *Doncaster Today* newspaper that he thought they wouldn't be safe: 'All I remember thinking was that we needed to smash our "save me" song so that we could stay in the competition. We don't know, from week to week, if we are going to get through because there's been a lot of surprises.'

When the boys left the stage, Niall jumped high in the air ('like a kangaroo', according to Louis) and they celebrated with their families.

Louis added: 'The pressure is really on, we've not had a minute. We're constantly working and improving our vocals. We've been doing eighteen-hour days and have been in the studio until 2am, so it's really tough. The boys deserved their place in the semi-final because they had put in two great performances. If they had gone out, it would have been a travesty.'

THE SING-OFF

Katie was automatically eliminated because she received the fewest votes. Wagner and Mary Byrne were in the sing-off: Wagner chose to sing 'Unforgettable' by Nat King Cole and Mary picked Shirley Bassey's 'This Is My Life'. Louis, Dannii and Cheryl chose to send Wagner home and so he became the eleventh act to leave the show.

S is for...

School

The boys loved the schools they went to before entering *The X Factor* and have each popped back several times to visit. During one of their *X Factor* video diaries, Zayn decided to do a shout out to Lowerfields Primary, his old school. All the boys really appreciate everyone who has supported them from day one: if their teachers hadn't backed them and encouraged them to be singers when they were at school, some members of the group might not be singing today!

In early November 2010, Louis made a very emotional trip to Willow Primary School in Doncaster.

The visit wasn't planned but as the children sat in assembly, Louis appeared. Three little girls in particular couldn't stop smiling: Phoebe, Daisy and Felicite were thrilled to see their big brother and gave him a massive hug. Phoebe and Daisy hadn't see him for eight weeks and so they couldn't take their eyes off him as he talked to the children about *The X Factor* and how you should always follow your dreams.

His mum explained what happened next to the *Star*: 'He didn't sing to them, but a few of the pupils sang to him – that was really nice. They asked him what he thought and he told them, he was very impressed. Later on he went on to Hayfield School to visit his old psychology teacher, Mr Cartledge. He went there before he did his A-levels at Hall Cross.

'There were girls shouting and screaming – I think they're more excitable at that age! He was signing autographs and having photos taken.'

Louis ended up having a very packed day off: he went to the cinema, signed autographs, went home, spent some time with the rest of his family, crawled into bed and then caught the 8.30 train back to London!

Liam is also grateful for the support his schoolmates have given him, before *The X Factor* and now. He went to St Peter's Collegiate School in Wolverhampton and left a lasting impression on all who knew him: brilliant at drama and sport, he also sang in the school choir.

Michael Coates used to sing in the same choir with Liam and when they were thirteen or fourteen, they entered a school talent competition together. They sang R. Kelly's 'If I Could Turn Back The Hands Of Time'. Until Year 8 or 9 not many people knew that Liam was a great singer, they just thought he was a runner. Michael and Liam are still really close and Michael was gutted when his friend didn't make *The X Factor* live shows in 2008. The two of them went to meet JLS with another friend called Sam when Marvin, Aston, JB and Oritsé were in Wolverhampton, doing a gig. Michael told the *Express & Star*: 'We went to their hotel, the Britannia. Liam told them we used to sing together and he got me to sing the R. Kelly song. I couldn't believe I was singing to JLS!'

All Liam's school friends are so proud of him and can't wait to see him perform on stage with One Direction. They knew he would make it one day.

Niall went to Coláiste Mhuire, which is an all-boys school and so he's not used to getting anywhere near as much attention as he's getting now from girls. The school were so pleased when One Direction made the live shows and put a special message up on their website to tell Niall they would be supporting him all the way. One of his friends from school – Graham Dowling – told the *Herald* newspaper: 'He's like a celebrity here, there are posters everywhere.' Graham has known Niall ever since they were five or six years old and says he's a born pop star.

Semi-final – Week Eight

In the semi-final, the final five acts had to perform two songs: the first had to be a Club Classic and the second was a 'Get-Me-To-The-Final' song. Basically, the second one could be any song they wanted to sing that would cause the people at home to pick up their phones and vote for them. All the acts wanted to be sure that they picked the right songs as they couldn't afford to mess up: everyone wanted to be in the final.

For Liam, Louis, Niall, Harry and Zayn this was the hardest week, not only because of the fact that it was leading up to the semi-final but also because Zayn received some terrible news and had to rush home. His grandad had passed away and the other boys were left to rehearse without him. Simon Cowell was ill and so they couldn't turn to him for support but thankfully, he left his friend Tim to watch over the boys and help them in any way that he could. Cheryl was also kind enough to help out in any way she could too.

Zayn managed to make it back in time and performed – which proved how much he wanted One Direction to make the final. Also, he didn't want to let the other boys down. Harry, Liam, Louis and Niall knew that he was hurting and so they just tried to be there for him, if he needed to talk.

WHO SANG WHAT

Matt Cardle – 'You've Got The Love' by Florence And The Machine and 'She's Always A Woman' by Fyfe DangerField

Rebecca Ferguson – 'Show Me Love' by Steve Angelo and 'Amazing Grace' (Susan Boyle version)

Cher Lloyd – 'Love The Way You Lie' by Eminem and 'Nothin' On You' by B.O.B

Mary Byrne – 'Never Can Say Goodbye' by Gloria Gaynor and 'The Way We Were' by Barbra Streisand

One Direction – 'Only Girl In The World' by Rihanna and 'Chasing Cars' by Snow Patrol

WHAT THE JUDGES THOUGHT

Performance One – 'Only Girl In The World'
Louis Walsh: 'Week after week, you're getting better and better, and you bring hysteria to the show. If there is any justice you will absolutely be in the final – you deserve to be in the final! I think you're the next big boy band and you know guys, I love the way you've gelled. I know you're best friends and you've got something special.'

Dannii Minogue: 'Guys, I hope you never let us down because I really wanna see you guys as the next big boy band. I have to say, some weeks you come out and I think it's very samey – that one was brilliant, you really stepped it up for the semi-finals. Brilliant!'

Cheryl Cole: 'Okay, first of all I'm gonna say: "I love you guys." This week, for me, I got to know you all a little bit better because your mentor wasn't here. I thoroughly enjoyed mentoring you – thank you for that opportunity – but that song for me was a little bit dangerous because it's so current right now as Rihanna's record that you have to completely make it like it was never, ever written for her, and I don't know if it quite worked for me but I don't think it makes a difference. I hope to see you in the final.'

Simon Cowell: 'Someone's being tactical [referring to Cheryl's comments]. I've got to tell you guys, I know this is going to sound a little bit biased but I thought the song was absolutely perfect for you because it is exactly what I liked about them – they didn't take the safe option. They chose something completely different: they had the guts to do it. I thought you looked current, sounded current and standing by what Cheryl said, you guys are just fantastic to work with. Can I just say, you hear all the applause and people at home might think you're safe but nobody is safe in this competition and I would urge anyone, please, if they want to see these boys in the final, please pick up the phone and vote for them because they deserve it.'

Performance Two – 'Chasing Cars'
Louis Walsh: 'Liam, Zayn, Niall, Harry and Louis, I know your names! Guys, there's something about this band: you've definitely got something special. I think you're the next big boy band, but I said that last week. I loved the song choice, I loved the whole styling, I love the fact that you're really good friends. There's a great vibe about you! If there's any justice, all the young kids will pick up their phones and they're going to vote One Direction... you deserve it!'

Dannii Minogue: 'Guys, you've got through a really tough week and that was such a classy, classy performance! You've just grown up in front of our eyes and we've never, ever had such a good band on *The X Factor*, so proud to see you form on this show.'

Cheryl Cole: 'I know me personally, all the crew, all the staff... everybody has grown so fond of you guys over the last few weeks. This week I was so impressed, you didn't have Zayn, Simon wasn't around, you showed a real level of maturity and you really deserve a place in the final.'

Simon Cowell: 'Guys, Tim who's been working with you all week told me that you made a decision this morning to get in at eight in the morning so you could give yourselves more rehearsal time and that's what it's all about. It's not about excuses, it's about having that great work ethic, picking yourselves up after what was a very tough week, and I said this before – I genuinely mean this – I am proud of you as people as much as I am artists. That was a great performance, good for you!'

WHAT THE BOYS THOUGHT

All the boys loved the reaction they got from the audience and were glad that people liked the fact that they took a risk doing Rihanna's 'Only Girl in the World'. They had worked so hard in rehearsals to make sure that both songs were equally as good. They didn't want to do one great song and one rubbish song. Niall enjoyed doing a fun song and then one that showed off their voices. Niall, Zayn and Louis definitely proved that they can sing.

They were so happy when they found out that they had made the final, but asked fans to keep voting for one more week. They really wanted to win!

THE SING–OFF

Mary and Cher had to sing for a place in the final. Cher picked Britney Spears' 'Everytime' for her sing-off song, while Mary went for the song that she sang in Week

One: 'It's a Man's Man's Man's World' by James Brown. Louis voted to save Mary, but the other three judges put Cher through to the final and so Mary became the thirteenth person to leave the show.

Simon Cowell

Liam, Louis, Zayn, Harry and Niall feel like they owe everything to their mentor, Simon Cowell. They are so grateful that he liked them all as individuals at their first auditions and then decided at Boot Camp to give them a second chance, even though their Boot Camp performances weren't strong enough for them to be soloists. Simon could have just let them leave and concentrated on the bands he already had, but he recognised something special in each of them and he didn't want to let them go. He gave them a chance and was impressed with their well-rehearsed version of Natalie Imbruglia's 'Torn'.

Simon's favourite member of One Direction is Harry because he feels a connection to him and if he wants the band to do something, he can just tell Harry and he'll speak to the others and make sure it happens. He thinks Harry has a great personality and is very likeable. The feeling is mutual and Harry says that if he could swap places with any of *The X Factor* judges, he would pick Simon because he is superpowerful. It's interesting to think what might have happened to One Direction if they had been given another mentor: they needed Simon because he was tough but fair with them and each week, he was always encouraging them to put on a better performance.

Louis told the official *X Factor* website what the real Simon Cowell is like. He said: 'People think he's really scary and intimidating, but he's just like a normal guy really. On a Sunday we stand backstage and have a chat with him. We can always talk to him about our performances and music, but we also talk to him about football and girls, and things like that.

'He's really supportive and very hands-on, and as well as being a good mentor, he's a great bloke to have a bit of banter with!'

The boys like joking around and gave Simon a unique present for his birthday. Harry revealed to the *Mirror*: 'For Simon Cowell's birthday we got him a birthday card and taped £2.50 into it. That's 50p from each of us – he can buy whatever he wants with it.'

Simon always had faith that Liam, Louis, Zayn, Niall and Harry could make it all the way to the final but when Aiden Grimshaw left in Week Six, he admitted that for him, it was a 'wake-up call'. After that, he committed even more time and energy to making sure One Direction wouldn't be leaving early – he wanted them to win!

Simon told Konnie Huq: 'They get on well, and they have steel in their eyes and that's what I look for in my artists – someone who is willing to work hard.

'Also, what I like about them is that behind the scenes they respect their fans. Whether it is raining or cold, they are always outside talking to them. That's always a good sign and I think they'll go far.'

Cheryl added: 'They've only been together for five minutes. If that's what they can produce now, they'll be incredible in five years!'

T is for...

Twitter

Harry, Zayn, Louis, Niall and Liam are all on Twitter and they have an official One Direction Twitter account, too. If you want the latest news on the band, from what they ate this morning to the last thing they said before they went to bed, then you need to follow them. They always try to answer as many questions from fans as possible and post up exclusive photos, too.

Harry is the most popular member of the band on Twitter, followed by Liam, Louis, Niall and Zayn. There are lots of people pretending to be the boys on Twitter, so make sure you aren't being fooled!

ZAYN MEETS A FAN
OUTSIDE *The X
Factor* STUDIOS.

Here are the Twitter addresses you need:

One Direction –
http://twitter.com/onedirection

Harry – http://twitter.com/harry_styles

Zayn – https://twitter.com/zaynmalik

Louis – https://twitter.com/Louis_Tomlinson

Niall – https://twitter.com/NiallOfficial

Liam – https://twitter.com/Real_Liam_Payne

Other interesting people connected to the boys, who you might want to follow:

Harry's sister Gemma –
http://twitter.com/GemmaAnneStyles

Harry's mum Anne –
https://twitter.com/anne42cox

Their vocal coach Savan –
https://twitter.com/Savan_Kotecha

U is for...

Underwear

In early November 2010, the *Sun* reported that Liam, Louis, Niall, Zayn and Harry might be releasing One Direction boxer shorts for boys and girls in the future. Now they have won *The X Factor*, it is only a matter of time before One Direction T-shirts, mugs, hoodies and pyjamas hit the shops. They might even end up with their own range of dolls one day.

When they lived in *The X Factor* house, the boys were forever leaving their boxers on the floor of the bedroom or in the bathroom. They each had favourite pairs – Harry liked to wear green ones for performances and Louis prefers the boxers with stars on that he got for the 'American Anthems' Sunday show.

When Louis found a hospital gown lying around backstage after the 'American Anthems' show, he put it on and went outside to wave to fans. After he came back inside, he 'accidentally' revealed his special boxers – which were tucked into his gown! The fans waiting there loved it and photographers took loads of photos so the picture of Louis in his boxers appeared in quite a few newspapers and magazines.

Liam, Zayn, Niall and Harry just smiled and walked alongside Louis – they think he's really funny. It would be great if they released a pack of five boxer shorts with each lads' name on one: fans could have Zayn Mondays, Liam Tuesdays, Niall Wednesdays… and so on. There are already unofficial boxer shorts for sale on eBay with 'I love Harry Styles' written on them, but fans would like the boys to release their own official ones.

Harry is known for walking round naked, but he does have a single gold thong that he likes to wear. It freaked the girls out in *The X Factor house* when he just appeared out of nowhere, with only his gold thong covering his modesty. He admitted to the *Mirror* at the time: 'My favourite party trick is to wear nothing but a gold thong in the house. My friend bought it for me for my birthday. The Belle Amie girls say I prance around the house in it. I'd say it's more of a slow, gentle stroll…'

V is for...

Vocal Coach

When Simon Cowell commented after Harry's first audition that he needed some vocal training, he couldn't have imagined he'd get the opportunity to work with a master like Savan Kotecha. Savan is the lead vocal coach for *The X Factor* and he's also an award-winning songwriter. He has written tracks for JLS, Britney Spears, Usher, Westlife, Leona Lewis and many more international stars. In total, 40 million albums with tracks he has written have been sold.

As well as being their vocal coach, Savan became a close friend of Harry, Louis, Niall, Liam and Zayn during *The X Factor* live shows and he will be staying in

The X-Factor vocal coach, Savan Kotecha.

touch with them. No doubt, he will be one of the songwriters brought in to help them write the tracks for their first album. He understands the boys and knows what sort of music they want to produce.

Savan was recently interviewed by Nisha from the website Of Indian Origin. She asked him who was his favourite 2010 *X Factor* contestant. He replied: 'I can't pick favourites!!! Ha-ha... It's been an interesting experience so far. I was asked by Simon to come in and help make sure the contestants sing like pop artists and are prepared for the "real world". I would say, I'm more of a vocal producer on the show rather than a very technical vocal coach: I'm approaching it like I would in the studio because for the first time they are selling the recordings of the songs on iTunes. I've been learning a lot about TV and what it's like to have a "real job" – it's been great!'

Savan has gained a lot of fans from the show as he started appearing in *The X Factor* backstage videos wearing funny wigs and messing around with the contestants. He wrote a great jokey song for One Direction called 'Vas happenin', boys.' The lyrics state that Harry needs to win *The X Factor* because he can't get a job and that his dad could be Mick Jagger. He tells how Niall was raised by leprechauns, Louis needs a boat, Liam looks sad when he sings and Zayn is the master of echoes. It's a funny song and the video of Savan performing it with the boys is definitely worth a look.

Having a good relationship with the boys and the other contestants was important for Savan because he wanted them to feel relaxed in his company. He thought that if they saw him as someone who liked having a laugh, they would be more open to giving new things a go and not be scared to make mistakes; he also wanted to help make *The X Factor* a fun experience for them.

There was a lot that Savan had to teach the boys in the beginning. Liam had had vocal training before, but not to the same level. One day when Savan wanted to teach Harry how to sing from his diaphragm and not his throat, so he got him to lie on his back. It really helps you relax and Savan says you need to breathe as you do when you're sleeping. If you want to hear Harry singing from the floor, check out the video on the official *X Factor* website. Savan hoped that Harry would have learnt an important lesson – even if it was a bit weird to sing lying on the floor.

Harry revealed: 'You can tell the difference when you stand up. I thought you were joking the first time you told me to lie on the floor, but I can see that it works now.'

Everyone who takes part in *The X Factor* knows that it's important to warm their voices up before they go onstage. If they didn't do this before a live show or performance, they might cause some serious damage to their 'instrument'. Louis likes to joke that to warm up his voice, he just shouts: 'WARM UP, WARM UP, WARM UP!' This isn't really what happens at all: the boys have now been taught by Savan and the rest of the vocal coach crew exactly what they need to do.

W is for...

White Eskimo

Before auditioning for *The X Factor*, Harry was in a band called White Eskimo. In his first *X Factor* interview, he told Dermot O'Leary: 'I'm in a band with my friends from school – White Eskimo. I'm the lead singer. We entered a Battle of the Bands' competition about a year and a half ago and we won. Winning Battle of the Bands and playing in front of that many people really showed me that's what I wanted to do. I got such a thrill when I was in front of people singing, it made me want to do more and more.'

Harry's best friend Will was actually the first person who recognised that he had such an amazing voice. He needed a singer for the band and the first person he thought of asking was Harry because they were best friends. Harry never really wanted to sing, but he gave it a go and the rest is history.

During practices, Will taught Harry a bit of guitar. Harry can also play the kazoo [small wind instrument] and he played the tambourine during some White Eskimo gigs. Their style of music was very different to One Direction's: they drew inspiration from blink 182. The band performed at lots of school assemblies and a wedding, too. In many ways it's a shame that you can only apply for *The X Factor* if you are a singer because Harry's bandmates were pretty talented musicians. Maybe they could play for One Direction when they do their own tour. Fans of both bands would like that.

Will is still Harry's best friend, even though Harry had to officially leave the band once he was placed in One Direction. All his former bandmates wanted One Direction to win *The X Factor*. The band has recently recruited two new members so they are still performing together. White Eskimo now consists of Will on drums, Sam (bass) and Mike (guitar and vocals). You should check out their fan page on Facebook to see some great photos of Harry performing and messing around with his mates. They are in the process of recording their demo and will be releasing tracks very soon.

X is for...

X Factor

X has to stand for *The X Factor* because without it, Harry, Zayn, Niall, Louis and Liam would never have found each other. They are grateful to the show, but the series should equally be grateful for them. Without our five favourite boys, *The X Factor* wouldn't have been half as entertaining and fewer people would have tuned in. One Direction captured the whole nation: they found fans not only in the UK and Ireland, but in Belgium, America and Spain, too. It won't be long before the boys will be cracking Europe and America because they are so talented.

When Louis Walsh was asked before the latest series

CHER LLOYD VISITS HER HOMETOWN IN PREPARATION FOR THE FINAL *X FACTOR* SHOWDOWN.

started what the *X Factor* is, he said: 'The X Factor is when someone walks into a room, sings and they have something unique, the attitude, personality and presentation all rolled into one and you watch them perform and think immediately you could sell records. David Bowie, Elton – people like that have the X Factor.' Louis can now add One Direction to the list: they definitely have the X Factor.

Y is for...

Yvie Burnett

As well as working with Savan Kotecha, the boys were also trained by *The X Factor*'s other vocal coach, Yvie Burnett. She told the *Daily Record* that One Direction are really talented: 'They look like stars and act like stars – they have got absolutely everything.'

Normally the boys play pranks on other people but one night during their *X Factor* rehearsals, they themselves were pranked. Yvie introduced them to Radio 1 DJ Chris Moyles and he joked that the whole competition was a fix and that One Direction would be leaving that night. Yvie joined in and poor Harry got confused and asked her: 'Are we leaving the competition

FORMER *X FACTOR* VOCAL COACH, YVIE BURNETT.

tonight?' Chris is sure that he fooled Harry

him think that he was going home!

The boys almost didn't get to work with Yvie B

shortly before the series started, she was replaced

Simon Cowell. She was gutted as she had worked on

the show for five years and is an expert in her field.

However, her replacement didn't last long, at which

point Simon apologised and asked her to come back.

Yvie's so glad she did because she got to work with

One Direction and the other great acts from *The X

Factor* 2010.

...him singing with One Direction then he ...have liked to become an actor. Before *The X* ...*tor*, he thought he would probably end up doing an English degree and become a teacher. Unlike the others, he isn't very musical and the only instrument that he can play is the triangle.

FIVE FASCINATING FACTS ABOUT ZAYN

His worst nightmare would be his pants falling down during a performance while he's farting! Yuck!

Zayn would like Freddie from *Skins* to play him, if a movie was made about the band

He was the X *Factor* contestant who spent the longest time in front of the mirror

If he could be any animal in the world, he would pick a lion

Justin Bieber has offered to give him dancing lessons.

Above: One Direction – Liam, Louis, Zayn, Harry and Niall – have their picture taken in between rehearsals for *The X Factor*.

Below: Harry meets and greets fans outside the TV studios in London.

Above: Guess who? One Direction hold aloft signs (and carrots!) given to them by their adoring fans.

Below left: Louis is from Doncaster, South Yorkshire, and is the oldest member of One Direction.

Below right: Liam is something of an *X Factor* veteran, having made it all the way through to the judges' houses in 2008.

Above: The boys pose for a photo in their own personal jumpsuits!

Below left: Louis, out and about in London between *X Factor* auditions.

Below right: Zayn steps out of a limousine as he arrives for a film première.

Above: The boys pose for a photo in between rehearsals for *The X Factor.*

Below left: Harry – nicknamed 'H' – is one of the most popular members of One Direction.

Below right: Niall, Liam and Louis smile for the cameras.